Wonder Dogs

Wonder Dogs

True Stories *of* Extraordinary Assistance Dogs

MAUREEN MAURER
with JENNA BENTON

Revell

a division of Baker Publishing Group
Grand Rapids, Michigan

Published by Revell
a division of Baker Publishing Group
PO Box 6287, Grand Rapids, MI 49516-6287
www.revellbooks.com

Printed in the United States of America

Library of Congress Cataloging-in-Publication Data
Names: Maurer, Maureen, 1961– author. | Benton, Jenna, author.
Title: Wonder dogs : true stories of extraordinary assistance dogs / Maureen Maurer
   with Jenna Benton.
Description: Grand Rapids : Revell, a division of Baker Publishing Group, 2021.
Identifiers: LCCN 2020058629 | ISBN 9780800739379 (paperback) | ISBN
   9780800740757 (casebound)
Subjects: LCSH: Service dogs. | Dogs—Therapeutic use. | Human-animal relationships.
Classification: LCC HV1569.6 .M358 2021 | DDC 362.4/048—dc23
LC record available at https://lccn.loc.gov/2020058629

Scripture quotations labeled KJV are from the King James Version of the Bible.

Scripture quotations labeled NIV are from THE HOLY BIBLE, NEW INTERNATIONAL VERSION®. NIV®. Copyright © 1973, 1978, 1984, 2011 by Biblica, Inc.® Used by permission. All rights reserved worldwide.

Unless otherwise noted, all photos are courtesy of Assistance Dogs of Hawaii.

A portion of the proceeds from the sales of this book go toward helping to provide assistance dogs for those in need.

Some names and details have been changed to protect the privacy of the individuals involved.

Published in association with Books & Such Literary Management, www.booksandsuch.com

21 22 23 24 25 26 27   7 6 5 4 3 2 1

To Mary King and Momo Monahan,
who shared our vision from the beginning

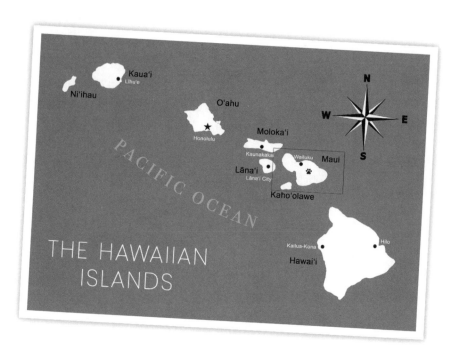

THE HAWAIIAN
ISLANDS

Kaua'i
Līhu'e
Ni'ihau
O'ahu
Honolulu
Moloka'i
Kaunakakai
Wailuku   Maui
Lāna'i
Lāna'i City
Kaho'olawe
Kailua-Kona
Hilo
Hawai'i
PACIFIC OCEAN

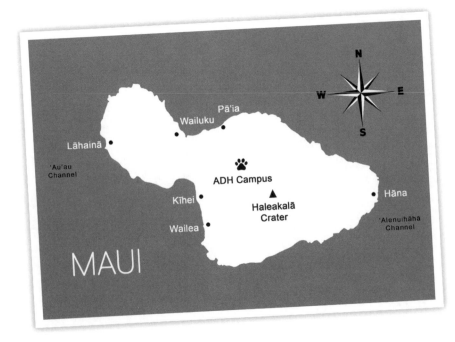

MAUI

Pā'ia
Wailuku
Lāhainā
'Au'au
Channel
ADH Campus
Kīhei
Haleakalā
Crater
Hāna
Wailea
'Alenuihāhā
Channel

Contents

Contents

Acknowledgments

Many people (and dogs) have helped *Wonder Dogs* become a book, and I am thankful for every one of them. First of all, my amazing husband, Will, who has helped to make all my dreams come true. None of this—our program, my career, or the book—would be possible without him. I'm eternally grateful for my late mom, who always encouraged me to reach for the stars (and finally let me have a dog!). I'm thankful for my sisters and our dad, who shared his love of dogs with us and always taught by example to help those in need. I'd be remiss if I didn't mention my own dogs, Sadie and Samson, who kept me company while I was writing this book and patiently answered my many questions.

Stephanie Hessemer and Robin Jones Gunn were the first to recognize the story in Assistance Dogs of Hawaii's mission. They introduced me to my wonderful agent, Janet Kobobel Grant, who has been a delight to work with. My gifted collaborator, Jenna Benton, has contributed her warmth and wisdom throughout the process and always made things fun.

This book wouldn't be possible without the talented team at Revell, especially my brilliant editors Vicki Crumpton and Kristin Adkinson.

My heartfelt appreciation goes out to the many friends who helped me along the way. Kristin von Kreisler graciously mentored me through the publishing process and provided inspiration, encouragement, and humor. Debbie Sutherland offered insightful advice and input (even though she is a cat person). My wonderful friend Michael Gartner lent his considerable editing expertise. Marsha Sarver managed to decipher my chicken scratch while patiently transcribing my drafts. I'd also like to thank Amanda Talarico, Kate McCoy, Merv Dorr, Kimmy Seguin, Grace Talarico, and Vanesa Vizuete for their invaluable input.

As I wrote, I felt the entire Assistance Dogs of Hawaii *ohana* right beside me: our graduates, who face unimaginable challenges with grace and courage; our assistance dogs, who go above and beyond to help their partners; and our dedicated volunteers and generous supporters, who make it all possible.

Most of all, I thank God for answering my prayers and giving me a second chance. I feel blessed to have found my purpose and am thankful for the opportunity to make a difference in the lives of others.

Maureen "Mo" Maurer

"Are you a dog lover?" Mo asked me during one of our early meetings.

I squirmed in my seat.

"I like dogs," I said carefully. "I was attacked by a dog when I was a kid, but I'm okay, and yeah . . . they're great."

Mo raised her eyebrows, smiled, and hired me anyway.

Mo encouraged me to learn everything I could about dogs. I sat in on puppy classes on Bainbridge Island and even experienced my very own "visits" and "snuggles" from dogs who were in training. I spent hours interviewing dog handlers and their families and was moved by their resiliency and the way they generously shared their stories. I wandered the halls of The Queen's Medical Center in Honolulu to observe hospital facility dogs in action and cried when I met Dr. Wendi and she told me stories about Tucker. I walked the Freedom Trail through the eucalyptus forest with Sadie, and it is as breathtaking as you'd imagine it might be. A good-natured golden retriever lay at my feet and let me dig my toes into his soft fur while I typed away at Mo's kitchen table. My mind and heart have been forever changed. Dogs truly are a gift to us all.

Just in case you're wondering, Mo and Will really are as incredible as you hope they are. They are tireless, brilliant, gracious, and fun. I will be forever grateful that the Maurers welcomed me into their world and call me their friend.

I'd like to thank my agent, Janet Kobobel Grant, for introducing me to Mo and this wonderful opportunity, and also our talented editor Vicki Crumpton for her encouragement and expertise. And to Cindy Coloma, thank you for endless friendship and solid advice.

To my family and friends, and also to my writing council, I hope these stories inspire you to lean into your own adventures. To my kids, thank you for pitching in and creating a beautiful space for me to write. I love being your mom. To my husband and best friend, David, I love you. I know for a fact I wouldn't be where I am without you. And to my mom, I wish you were here to read this one. I'll miss you forever.

Oh, and guess what? I AM A DOG LOVER.

Jenna Benton

1

Tucker Finds His Calling

There are only two ways to live your life. One is as though nothing is a miracle. The other is as though everything is a miracle.

Albert Einstein

CHRISTMAS 2005

The warm tropical air breezed through Kahului Airport, welcoming crowds of bustling travelers to Maui. The vacationers made their way through open-air walkways and down the escalator to baggage claim, pointing and smiling as they caught glimpses of the whitecapped Pacific Ocean and palm trees along the way. Hawaiian music filled the air and the sweet scent of plumeria lei drifted toward me as I sat on a concrete bench in the baggage claim area and stared at the cargo door.

I could hardly contain my excitement. I was about to welcome a special visitor of my own to our island home.

With a loud click, the heavy metal door slowly opened, and I jumped to my feet. A man walked out carrying a small airline kennel and smiled as he approached. He carefully placed the kennel on the ground, and I crouched down to look inside. Staring back at me from behind the wire door was the most beautiful golden retriever puppy I'd ever seen. He had a big head, like a Saint Bernard's, and a fluffy golden coat. His dark brown eyes shone with a friendly and intelligent expression.

"Hello, my friend," I said as I squeezed the metal latch to open the kennel door. He stepped out, surprisingly self-composed after traveling all the way from Australia. He stood calmly and smiled up at me with his bright eyes and slowly wagged his tail. I had seen a lot of puppies over the years but knew in that moment he was going to be something special. However, I never could have imagined the way Tucker was going to change my life and impact the world around him.

As we drove home, I struck up a conversation with Tucker and told him all about my husband, Will. I also briefed him on his new classmates and the adventures he was going to have while learning to be an assistance dog. Instead of looking out the window, Tucker stared intently back at me and listened to every word. He made me feel like the most fascinating person in the world. We followed the winding gravel road past tall palm trees and lush vegetation to our little beachside cottage.

We pulled into our driveway and I opened the car door and lifted Tucker to the ground. He was a solid puppy and surprisingly heavy for only ten weeks old. He looked up at me with a smile and cocked his head as if to say, *What's next?*

Courtesy of Kathryn Reiger

Tucker at 10 weeks old

"It looks like Will isn't home yet. Would you like to go to the beach?" I asked.

Tucker wagged his tail in response and followed me into the cottage, where I changed into my swimsuit. Our shingled one-bedroom cottage stood at the edge of a crescent-shaped turquoise bay that was fringed with a white sandy beach. It was a sanctuary for us during the early years of launching our fledgling nonprofit.

Tucker and I followed the short path to the beach, and I kicked off my flip-flops next to a palm tree. I took a deep breath of the salt air as I stretched out my toes in the powdery sand. The sky above was clear blue, but billowy clouds nestled along the horizon as they waited for the sun to settle in for the night. We had the beach all to ourselves and walked toward the shallow water. It was Tucker's first experience of the ocean, and he sniffed at the bubbly white foam that left a crooked little trail along the water's edge. He sat down and watched as I waded out into the water. I looked back at Tucker, who had just discovered his first coconut. He pounced on it and paraded up and down the beach, carrying it in his mouth. I laughed out loud and he wagged his tail in reply.

"I see you, Tucker," I called and waved. The coconut was almost as big as he was, and when he tried to shake it back and forth, the momentum was too much, and he fell over and rolled down the sand. He stood up and shook himself off, quickly restoring his dignity. He placed an oversize paw on the coconut to hold it still and began to methodically peel back the fibrous husk.

Seeing him so happily occupied, I took a deep breath and dove into the clear blue water. Its coolness instantly covered my skin. When I popped back up, I saw that Will had arrived home and was playing with Tucker on the beach. He tossed the coconut and Tucker pranced back to him, carrying it in his mouth.

Will was wearing red surf shorts and waved as he saw me coming out of the water. "What a great puppy. I can't believe he's already retrieving!" He bent down and held Tucker's head in his hands. "Welcome to our *ohana*, little fella."

Will carried his surfboard toward the shore as Tucker toddled after him with the coconut in his mouth. He stopped just short of the water's edge and looked at Will with a hopeful expression on his face. I stepped out of the water and bent down to pet Tucker. He certainly was the perfect addition to our *ohana*, our family.

"There's something very special about this puppy," I said. "I think he may be the best one we've ever had."

"You say that about all of them," Will teased. His blue eyes twinkled as he leaned down and gave me a kiss before paddling out toward the waves.

"And I'm always right!" I shouted after him, laughing.

I sat on the beach and Tucker curled up next to me. I stroked the downy fur on his head and noticed his ears were a little darker gold than the rest of his coat. They had tiny waves that looked like they'd been crimped with a curling iron. He rested his chin on my knee as we watched Will catch a few waves. The horizon began to glow with orange and pink streaks where the water met the sky.

"There is something special about you, Tucker," I said, as he snuggled in a little closer. "I can't wait to see what your calling in life will be."

I picked up a handful of sand and noticed the subtle colors of the tiny grains as they fell slowly through my fingers. They reminded me of a poem I liked by William Blake called "Auguries of Innocence":

> To see a World in a Grain of Sand
> And a Heaven in a Wild Flower,
> Hold Infinity in the palm of your hand
> And Eternity in an hour.

It had been five years since I'd sold my CPA practice and taken a leap of faith to follow my childhood dream of training assistance dogs. For the first time in my life, I felt like I was fulfilling my purpose and was exactly where I was meant to be. Several dogs had already graduated from our program and were thriving with newfound purpose and making a difference in the world. We currently had four heroes-in-training, and I couldn't wait to introduce Tucker to his classmates the next day. The sun was just setting as Will paddled back to shore. He carried his surfboard in one arm and picked up the sleeping Tucker in the other. I carried Tucker's prized coconut as we headed back to our cottage with growling stomachs and full hearts.

We rinsed off the salt water in the outdoor shower and Will dried Tucker off with a beach towel. We sat outside out on the lanai as the sky darkened to a deep blue and stars began to appear overhead. Will set bowls of puppy food and water on the floor, and Tucker eagerly finished both of them. We laughed as he licked the food bowl clean and then pushed it around the lanai with his nose. I sat in the hammock as Will fired up the grill for dinner.

Will and I had met at a neighborhood barbecue almost twenty years before. I was a business student at Seattle University, and he had just graduated as a mechanical engineer from the University of Washington. From the moment I first saw Will walk through the door, I had the strangest feeling—not that I recognized him, but that I *knew* him. It was a sense of déjà vu that I'd never experienced before. Looking at him standing in the doorway, it was as if I had a glimpse of memories yet to come. He just saw a girl gawking at him, but thankfully he decided to come over and say hello.

Although I was initially charmed by his good looks, it was his faithfulness and steadfast love that captured my heart. We both enjoyed adventure and explored the world together. Sometimes we traveled just for fun, like when we rented a campervan and toured New Zealand for a month. Usually, our trips had more purpose, like the time we volunteered with Habitat for Humanity to rebuild houses in Fiji after a hurricane, or the time we went with our church to bring supplies to refugees during the war in Croatia. We moved to Maui right after college because of our love of ocean sports and the outdoors. We also worked hard to build successful careers. In every adventure, in every season, Will was my partner.

When I woke up the next morning, Will had already gone to work. There was a gardenia and a note from him on my nightstand that said he'd already fed Tucker and taken him for a walk. I leaned over the bed and saw Tucker lying on his back on the dog bed, his big paws twitching in his sleep. His tail was wagging and I wondered what he was dreaming about. After breakfast, I loaded Tucker into the car, and we drove to our office so he could begin the first step in his long journey to becoming an assistance dog.

Our program operated out of donated retail space in the Queen Kaʻahumanu Center, an open-air shopping mall in Kahului. My dream was to eventually build a permanent campus that would last for generations, but for now there were many advantages to this location. Having an office in the mall meant we could practice with the puppies on elevators, escalators, and in the movie theater. It was also a great training ground for navigating noisy crowds, shops, and restaurants. Tucker's first day at work coincided with Christmas decorations being put up in the mall. My heart soared as I saw the huge Christmas tree being decorated. This was my favorite time of year.

We entered our small office, and Donna, our office manager, greeted us with a big smile. I placed Tucker on the ground and four puppies came scrambling over to meet him. Tucker stood his ground and slowly wagged his tail as he was thoroughly inspected by his new classmates.

At eight months old, Oliver was the ringleader. He was a big yellow lab and the life of the party wherever he went. Penny, a sweet and unassuming black lab about the same age, was a gentle soul. Whenever the dogs played too rough, she quickly excused herself to lie under a desk. The two other puppies, Riggins and Riley, were energetic yellow labs and littermates who were six months old. They quickly formed a racetrack around the small office, chasing Oliver, who was playing keep-away with his favorite pink elephant. Oliver encouraged Tucker to play by shoving the toy in his face. I smiled as I pictured what our little cottage would be like when it was bursting at the seams with all these puppies over the holidays.

We usually went home to Seattle for Christmas, but this year our volunteer puppy raisers (the families who foster the puppies) were all on vacation and there was no one else to watch them. I didn't mind. There were a lot worse things than being stuck on a tropical island with a bunch of adorable puppies for Christmas.

A week later, Will and I sat on our couch as the five puppies played with their toys and gently gnawed on each other's limbs. We were trying to decide how we would celebrate our first Christmas alone. My mom used to have my sisters and me think of a birthday present for Jesus each year, and I liked to carry on that tradition. Remembering my early childhood suddenly gave me an idea.

"Why don't we take one of the puppies to visit the children's hospital on Oahu? Remember our last visit and how much it cheered everyone up?"

"That's a great idea," said Will. "Which one should we take?"

The older puppies were now chasing each other around the living room, and I tried unsuccessfully to picture them in a hospital setting. I shook off the mental image and looked down at the youngest puppy sitting calmly at my feet.

"Let's take Tucker. He's the gentlest one of all. Plus, he looks like a real, live teddy bear. The children will love him!"

Soon it was Christmas morning. We woke up early to open presents and stockings and then settled Tucker into the car and drove to the airport to catch the forty-minute flight to Honolulu. My fear of flying was second only to my fear of public speaking, but I was starting to get more comfortable with the short interisland flights I often had to take for work. Part of Tucker's training included exposure to new environments, so traveling with us in the cabin and visiting the big city would be a great learning opportunity for him. I couldn't wait for the children to meet Tucker and was curious to see how he would respond to all the distractions in a hospital setting.

We parked outside and walked through the sliding hospital doors into the air-conditioned lobby of Kapiolani Medical Center. Tucker had fallen asleep in Will's arms and looked adorable in his blue puppy coat. Since it was Christmas morning, a single receptionist replaced the usual crowds in the lobby and activity at the front desk.

"Merry Christmas," Will said with a smile. "This is Tucker, and we're here for a therapy visit with the patients."

The woman glanced up from her computer and her eyes went straight to Tucker. He wore a fluffy red-and-white Christmas collar around his neck, and the little bells sewn around the edges jingled softly as he shifted in Will's arms and woke up.

"Oh my goodness! That is the cutest puppy I've ever seen. He looks like a stuffed animal. I'm just sorry there aren't more children here today to see him," she said. "All of the patients who were well enough went home to spend Christmas Day with their families. The only ones still here are from off-island or those who are too sick to leave."

I suddenly realized this visit might not be what I had imagined. But then I thought of how Tucker would bring some much-needed joy to the children who remained. Even if we made a difference for just one patient today, it would be well worth the trip.

"It's okay," I piped up. "We would love to visit with the children who are here."

"Great! Go on up to the fifth floor." The woman pointed to the elevator across the lobby. "I'll let the nurses' station know you're on your way up. Bye, Tucker!"

As Will pressed the button for the elevator, I said a quick prayer. *Lord, please let us be a blessing to these children, and lead us to the ones who are most in need.*

I opened my eyes and watched the numbers above the elevator light up as it made its way down to us in the lobby. I mentally prepared myself for what we were about to see. I reminded myself to be a ray of sunshine for the children, no matter how sad or serious their conditions might be.

The doors opened, and Will put his hand on my back as we stepped into the elevator. Will. My rock. We had been on this adventure for so long I knew I didn't need to say a word. He smiled at me reassuringly, knowing how I felt about hospitals after spending so much time in them myself. I pressed the button for the fifth floor. Tucker looked at me contentedly from the safety of Will's strong arms as the elevator started to climb. I smiled at Tucker and stroked his big head as his soulful brown eyes stared into mine.

As the elevator doors slid open, we stepped into the bright hallway and immediately heard a squeal of delight as the first child had already spotted Tucker.

"Ohhh, he's so cute. Is he real?" asked the little boy. I smiled at him and the nurse who was pushing his wheelchair. She looked almost as excited as her patient. Will assured him that Tucker was indeed real and asked if he would like to pet him.

"Yes, please. My dog is at home and I miss her so much."

Will gently placed Tucker down, and he melted onto the boy's lap. The boy stroked his soft fur as Tucker rested his chin on the armrest of the wheelchair. Myriad questions tumbled out.

"What's his name? How old is he? Why is he wearing a blue coat?" asked the boy with excitement.

"His name is Tucker," I said. "And he's twelve weeks old. He's wearing the blue coat because he's in training to be a special dog who will help people when he grows up." Tucker looked up at the little boy's face and gently wagged his tail.

"Well, I think he'll be really good at his job because he's already helping me!"

After a few more minutes of visiting with the boy, we continued down the hallway. "Tucker, my friend," I whispered to him, "I have a feeling this may be your calling."

We walked by a private room and I looked through the window to see if the occupants might like a visit. There was a young woman sitting next to a hospital bed. A little girl lay motionless on the bed and was connected to several machines. The woman held her daughter's hand, and I watched as she gently rocked from side to side, brushing away quiet tears. She looked up and our eyes met. I had never seen a look of such sadness, and I felt embarrassed for intruding. A nurse came hurrying over.

"I'm sorry, this patient is sleeping," she said. "But there's another patient in room 526 who would like a visit."

The nurse led us down the hall toward another room. I glanced back and saw the young mom watching us from the doorway as we walked away. My heart ached for her.

We visited several patients, and Tucker seemed to instinctively know what each child needed in the moment. Sometimes he lay completely still and other times he rolled over and wiggled, coaxing a giggle or two. Will and I were amazed at his confidence and the instant connection he seemed to have with the patients, their parents, and even the staff.

We were chatting with a nurse in the hallway when the young mother we had seen earlier walked up to us.

"Could you bring the puppy in to see my daughter?" she asked.

I looked over at the nurse to see if it was okay.

"Yes, but just for a couple of minutes," she said.

I took a deep breath and followed Will and the woman into the room.

Will carried Tucker to the girl's bedside and pulled up a chair next to her. Her frail body lay motionless. I tried not to look at all the machines that were monitoring her vitals.

"Liliana loved dogs more than anything in the world," the young mother said as she stroked her daughter's hair. My chest tightened and I fought back tears as I heard her speak of her daughter in the past tense. I almost couldn't bear the sadness.

She bowed her head and shared with us that Lili had an incurable disease and had not responded to anything in weeks. "She was taken off life support two days ago," she whispered.

"I'm so sorry," I replied, wishing I could think of something better to say. Will leaned in toward Lili with Tucker in his arms. The woman placed her daughter's hand on Tucker's head, guiding it, as she stroked his soft fur. We all watched in silence. Tucker was completely calm, but his twinkling brown eyes stared intently at Lili's face.

The sound of steady beeping from the machine above her head suddenly grew faster. I glanced up at the screen and noticed that the zigzag line on the heart monitor was changing too. I looked at Lili, whose hand was still resting on Tucker's ear. Almost imperceptibly, her fingers began to move. Her mother stared in disbelief as we watched Lili move her fingertips over Tucker's ear. "NURSE, NURSE!" the mom's shout echoed down the hallway.

"What is it?" a nurse asked as she rushed in and checked the screens above the bed.

"She's moving!" cried the mother. "Her hand. LOOK!"

We all looked—Liliana's fingers were deliberately touching the crimped hair on Tucker's ear. The nurse's eyes widened as she checked the numbers on the screen and pushed a button attached to the bed. Suddenly there was commotion everywhere, as doctors were paged, and more hospital staff came rushing into the room. Will picked up Tucker, who smiled at Lili and seemed unfazed by all the activity.

"I'm sorry, you'll have to leave," said the nurse as she herded us toward the door.

"Wait," said the mom. She came over and hugged Tucker as tears spilled down her cheeks onto his soft fur. "Thank you, Tucker. You're our Christmas miracle."

Will and I moved to the end of the hallway so we would be out of the way. I took a deep breath and looked at Will, whose blue eyes brimmed with tears. He took my hand, and we prayed for Lili as the doctors and nurses gathered in her room.

We visited a few more patients before it was time to leave. As we passed the nurses' station on the way back to the elevator, I caught a flash of neon yellow out of the corner of my eye and saw that there was a sign taped to a door that read "ISOLATION—Do Not Enter." Looking through the window, I saw a small hospital bed that was enclosed in a clear plastic tent. It contained a young girl, who was staring up at the ceiling.

"I'm sorry," a nurse called from the station. "That patient is in isolation and can't have any visitors."

"Would it be okay if we just showed her Tucker through the window?" I asked.

"That's fine," she replied as she returned to her phone call.

Will held Tucker up to the glass and smiled at the little girl through the window. Her body shifted under the blanket, and she turned her head our way, trying to focus. Her eyes widened as she saw Tucker in his Christmas costume. Will waved one of Tucker's big paws at the girl, who looked to be about five years old. A faint smile appeared on her face. It wasn't the biggest smile I had ever seen, but it was the most beautiful.

As we waved goodbye to the patient in the isolation room, I suddenly noticed my own reflection in the glass. Distant memories came flooding back. I knew exactly how she felt, because I had once been that little girl . . .

Tucker comforting a patient

2

Samba Sparks Wonder

"For I know the plans I have for you," declares the Lord, *"plans to prosper you and not to harm you, plans to give you hope and a future."*

Jeremiah 29:11 NIV

July 1968

The light from seven candles danced on the white frosted cake as my mother walked carefully into the dining room and my family began to sing. My heart skipped a beat at the thought of having to blow out the candles. My lungs were stronger than last year, but there would be one more candle to blow out. Mom placed the cake in front of me as everyone finished the song's last verse, the one that always made my sisters and me laugh: *Happy birthday to you. You look like a monkey, and you smell like one too!*

"Make a wish," my mom said with a smile.

I didn't have to think about what to wish for. I had recently concluded that if I always wished for just one thing, it would be more likely to come true. So, I decided every birthday wish and every wish upon a star would be the same. My wish wasn't for healthy lungs or to spend less time in the hospital. My wish was simple. I wanted to talk to animals like Doctor Dolittle, the hero of my favorite book. Deep in my heart I believed that one day, if I wished hard and often enough, my dream would come true. I kept this a secret because I'd heard if you told anyone your wish, it would never happen. I squeezed my eyes shut.

I wish to talk to animals, I prayed. I opened my eyes and studied the placement of the candles on the cake and came up with a plan. I pictured the breathing machine I used and how the nurse taught me to exhale as hard as I could to get the ball to rise to the top of the tube. I concentrated and drew in the biggest breath I could manage. I began to blow and counted each candle as it went out—four, five, six. I was doing it! The seventh candle still flickered, and I was running out of breath. I started getting dizzy as I pushed out the last bit of air from my lungs.

"You did it!" my mom cheered. Too exhausted to reply, my huge smile said it all.

As the months passed, I slowly became stronger and healthier. There were still many days when my asthma and allergies caused me to stay home alone while my parents were at work and my sisters were at school. On the weekends, I lost myself in the piles of books I brought home from the library. I was a tomboy and loved the outdoors, especially playing in the rustic tree house my dad built in the backyard. I usually had it all to myself, since my sisters preferred playing together inside.

The days when I was well enough, I walked to the Green Lake Library and brought home as many books as I could carry. Mrs. Palmer, the librarian, knew my name. She was always so nice to me and knew exactly what I was looking for. She let me know every time they received a new children's book about dogs, and she set them aside for me behind her desk.

I was infatuated with all the Lassie stories and the series about Lad the dog, but my favorite continued to be the story of Doctor Dolittle. I read it so many times, I could practically recite it by heart. The idea that someone could talk to animals sparked something deep inside me, and I wanted more than anything to communicate with animals as he did.

One night I was in bed reading a book I had just gotten called *Follow My Leader*. It was about a boy my age who was blind and received a guide dog named Leader. A girl I knew from the hospital was also blind, and the story reminded me of her. I was captivated by the book and couldn't put it down, even though it was long past my bedtime.

"Mo," my mother called up the stairs. "Are you reading under the covers again? If you keep doing that, you're going to go blind."

I quickly switched off my flashlight and stared at the ceiling in excitement. If I were to go blind, could I get a guide dog? I fell asleep dreaming of what it would be like to have a dog of my own.

The next morning during breakfast, I asked my mom if I could get a guide dog if I went blind from reading under the covers.

"No," she laughed. "Chances are, you won't ever need a guide dog, but perhaps when you're older, you can train them to help others."

I stared at my mother wide-eyed. This was the best thing I'd ever heard! At that moment I knew that when I grew up, I wanted to train dogs to help people. I thought about my wish to talk to animals and how much it would help in my future career.

"You're going to be late for school, Mo," my mom said, glancing at the clock on the wall. I kissed her goodbye and hurried out the front door.

"Mo, wait!" my mom called when I had almost reached the sidewalk. "Don't forget your backpack."

I raced back and grabbed it from her outstretched arm. She laughed at me and shook her head as I headed back out the door and ran all the way to school. My mind was bursting with ideas about how dogs could help people.

That summer, my mom gathered my sisters and me on the couch one afternoon and explained that my dad was not going to live with us anymore. She said that while they both loved us very much, sometimes grown-ups had to live apart. Part of our new normal was transitioning from St. Benedict's to a large public school. This was a challenge for me, since I was small and painfully shy. I also had a droopy eye that some kids liked to make fun of. I began third grade at the new school and found the classwork was easy, so I often sat at my desk daydreaming about dogs.

Many days I still stayed home, sitting in front of the humidifier that helped me breathe and watching reruns of *Lassie*. Whenever I was well enough, I walked more than a mile along the busy city streets to my new school and knew every dog along the route. I occasionally tried talking to some of the friendlier ones, just to see if my wish had come true yet. Although they wagged their tails and always looked happy to see me, none of them ever talked back. I taught myself to whistle in an attempt to communicate better with them.

I desperately wanted a dog of my own, so I befriended every stray dog I encountered and tried to coax them to follow me home. I couldn't resist petting them and burying my fingers in their fur. I eventually arrived home with swollen eyes, sneezing uncontrollably, and begged my mom to keep the dog. Exasperated, she always said no and reminded me that I was severely allergic to dogs. I learned to keep my hands away from my face after petting a dog and to wash them as soon as I got home.

I began to pray earnestly that my allergy to dogs would disappear. I even offered to strike a deal with God, letting him know I would be okay with having an allergy to all other animals, just not dogs. I was eventually taken to see an allergist. Dr. Brown was a nice older man, and I liked him immediately because of his crinkly eyes and the picture on his desk of his cute dog. Dr. Brown sent my mom home with a brown paper bag full of syringes, needles, and allergy serum. My mom practiced on an orange until she built up enough courage to give me my first injection. I tried to be brave so she wouldn't feel so nervous about giving me the shots.

One crisp fall day, my fingers brushed against an old chain-link fence as I walked home from school. I was daydreaming about all the things I would say to dogs if only I could talk to them.

Suddenly, I heard a ferocious growl from the other side of the fence and felt something touch my hand. I screamed and jumped back in terror. A big German shepherd was lunging and snapping wildly at me, his bared teeth pushing against the fence. Scared half to death, I ran the rest of the way home in tears.

I was terrified to walk to school after that, but my mom explained that the dog was probably scared of me too, which is why he acted that way. I found this hard to believe and the next day moved to the other side of the street well before I reached that block. I gave the shepherd a wide berth and watched him from afar for the next few days as I tiptoed down the street. He lived in an overgrown yard next to an old, dilapidated house. He was tethered by a short chain and barely had enough room to walk around his doghouse. I noticed he did look kind of scared, and maybe even sad.

"Hi there, fella," I called one day from across the street. He barked at the sound of my voice, and I quickly looked for a nearby tree to climb, just in case he broke through the fence. He stopped barking and I inched a little closer. Was that fear I saw in his eyes?

"Don't be scared. I won't hurt you. You're a good boy, aren't you?"

"Woof," he replied.

It sounded like yes to me, and my hopes lifted. Maybe my wish had finally come true! I tried to think of something else I could ask him. He looked so skinny that I could see his ribs sticking out from beneath his matted coat.

"Are you hungry?" I asked.

He looked directly at me but didn't say a word. Hiding my disappointment, I tried again.

"Would you like something to eat?"

He looked at me hopefully and appeared to be on the verge of speech. Instead, he whined just a little, which I again took as a yes.

"Okay, let me see what I have for you," I responded eagerly.

I looked in my Snoopy lunch pail for something to share and gingerly handed him half of a cheese sandwich through the chain link. He gulped it right down.

"You are hungry!" I exclaimed triumphantly.

I realized then that dogs don't have to speak in human voices for us to understand them. They have many other ways of communicating with us. My new friend spoke volumes through his facial expressions, vocalizations, posture, and movement.

As the days grew shorter and the air grew colder, our friendship grew deeper. I visited the big shepherd twice a day and named him Leader after the guide dog in my book. I'm not sure which one of us enjoyed our visits more. I still carried most of the conversation, but my understanding of his language was improving as I learned to recognize his different expressions and moods. I could tell when he was happy by the way he wagged his tail. I knew that when he gently nudged my hand through the fence, he was asking for a scratch behind the ears. I could tell he had a question when his eyebrows moved back and forth. Mostly I learned what he was thinking and feeling by the way he looked at me. His eyes seemed to reach into my soul, and I knew he was happy to finally have a friend.

Each day, he put his paws up on the fence and wagged his tail when he saw me coming a block away. Although I always brought something to share with him, I noticed he just kept getting skinnier.

There was snow on the ground when I woke up one morning, and I worried about Leader sleeping outside. How cold he must be! I dressed quickly and ran to his yard to check on him. When I arrived, he got up slowly and shook off the snow. I gave him some breakfast cereal that I'd snuck out of the house. His body shivered violently as he ate from my hand. I promised him I would be back after school and started planning right away what I would save for him from my lunch.

When I returned that afternoon, he wasn't waiting at the fence like usual.

"Here, Leader!" I called.

I had never seen his owner but thought perhaps someone had taken him inside to warm him up. I called out for him again just to make sure, but there was no response.

That's when I spotted him. A dark furry figure lay in the snow next to his doghouse. I called out to him, but he didn't move. I dropped my lunch pail and backpack and quickly climbed over the fence. I had never dared to venture inside the yard before, but this was an emergency. I had to help. I leaned in close to his face and whispered to him. I stroked his body and rocked him a little, trying to wake him, but he felt so cold and still.

"Wait right here, boy, I'll be back soon," I whispered in his ear before I clambered back over the fence.

I sprinted toward home as fast as my skinny legs could carry me. There was no time to waste. I returned a few minutes later with the scratchy wool blanket from my bed. I brushed away the snow that was covering his face and wrapped him in the blanket. Falling on my knees in the muddy snow, I rubbed the blanket with both hands, trying to warm him and wake him up. Eventually I lay down beside him, hoping to feel him breathe.

I'm not sure how long I lay next to him, but it was dark when my mom found me. My eyes were swollen shut and my breathing was shallow and wheezy. She gently wrapped me up in the blanket and carried me home. I was sick for days and inconsolable over the loss of my best friend. Even though I was young, I recognized the tragedy not only of his death but also of his life. My heart was broken into pieces.

A few weeks later, my mom came home from an errand and looked happier than I had seen her in a long time. She said she had a surprise for me and asked me to close my eyes. A surprise . . . for me?! I could barely contain my excitement as she took my arm and led me outside.

"Okay, you can open your eyes now!" she exclaimed.

Sitting on our front porch was a brown wicker basket. I lifted the lid and couldn't believe my eyes—there was a puppy inside! He had curly black hair that covered his face and a little white beard and a white star on his chest. His whole body wiggled with excitement when I said hello. I kept my hands behind me and looked up at my mom, biting my lip.

"Go ahead," she urged. "He's a toy poodle mix and is hypoallergenic. That means you can touch him. He has special hair that won't make you sneeze."

This was the best day ever! I reached out in amazement and picked him up. I buried my face in his silky coat and silently thanked God for answering my prayers. I named the puppy Samba, and we became inseparable. I loved his soft hair, but the length of it kept us from seeing each other clearly. One of my sister's hair clips did the job to keep his hair out of his eyes. And what eyes they were! They were black and bright and full of life, and absolutely shone with intelligence.

I couldn't wait to show Samba the tree house, but although he tried, he wasn't able to follow me up the wooden boards that were nailed to the trunk. Each time I went up, he barked and looked up at me, frantically wagging his tail. I tried to carry him in one arm and climb with the other, but he wiggled too much. Finally, I wore my backpack on the front and put Samba inside. His black curly head was all that appeared above the zipper, and we were nose to nose as we ascended the tree. Samba loved being in the tree house, so I decided to decorate it and make it more homey for us. He supervised and encouraged my progress from above as I made several trips up and down the ladder. I carried up a folding lawn chair, some books, a flashlight, a blanket, and a bucket for our table, along with his water bowl, tennis ball, and squeaky toy. We spent many happy afternoons reading books, playing fetch, and sharing secrets. When it was getting dark, my mom would call us in for dinner. Getting down was much easier, as there was a long plastic slide that my dad had salvaged from an old play set. Samba sat on my lap while we flew down the slide and returned to earth together.

One day on the way home from school, I saw a sign on a telephone pole advertising a dog obedience class. I asked my mom if Samba and I could enroll in the twelve-week class. I was surprised when she said yes, since I knew we didn't have much money for extra things. I took the class very seriously, and Samba and I practiced our homework every day after school. I was astonished to discover that I was the only child in the class, since I was still painfully shy, especially around adults. Samba helped me come out of my shell, and I was much more comfortable speaking to adults by the end of the three months. I was also much more comfortable around dogs. I wasn't sure if it was my prayers or the allergy shots, but by the end, I could pet all the other dogs in the class without sneezing!

The last week of class was an obedience competition. Each student demonstrated what their dog had learned, including

Mo at 7 years old

Samba at 3 months old

"heel," "sit," "down," "stay," "shake," and "come here." During the awards ceremony on the last day, Samba received a blue ribbon for the most improved dog. Everyone clapped and I was so proud of Samba that I burst into tears.

Since Samba already knew everything we had learned in the class, I decided to teach the other dogs in our neighborhood. I made a flyer for free dog training lessons and put one in the mailbox of every neighbor who had a dog. I was thrilled when our phone rang the next day with someone wanting to sign up. I had my first customer!

Eventually I had five students, ranging from the Petersons' twelve-year-old Maltese named Coco from across the street to the Carters' six-month-old Great Dane puppy named Duke from down the block. I loved my students and hurried home from school each day so I could teach them all to sit, roll over, and stay. Samba was my assistant and helped the slower dogs by patiently demonstrating the commands for them.

In preparation for the final day of class, I cleared a big round space on the empty lot next door and set up a ring for a dog show. I passed out handwritten invitations to the entire neighborhood. The big day arrived, and the dogs' owners took turns walking them on a leash around the circle and giving them commands. I scored them just like I had seen the instructor in class do with Samba. At the end, I added up the points and awarded first prize to Coco. Mrs. Peterson smiled and was so proud of her dog as they came up to get the ribbon, and Mr. Peterson said it proved that you could teach an old dog new tricks. This made everyone laugh!

One weekend after the dog show, my sisters and I were camping out on the living room floor in our sleeping bags. It was late, and as my sisters slept soundly on either side of me, I lay awake thinking about Samba. He was such a smart puppy and always seemed to know exactly what I wanted, sometimes even before I said a word. *Maybe he can read my mind*, I thought.

I decided to test this theory as I watched him sleeping under the dining room table. I closed my eyes and thought as hard as I could about the word *stand*. I opened my eyes and was astonished to see Samba now standing in the spot where he had been sleeping. I squeezed my eyes tightly and pictured him again in my mind.

Come here! I silently asked him.

I opened my eyes and discovered him standing right in front of me, his shining dark eyes looking right into mine. I couldn't believe it! Somehow, Samba had heard my thoughts.

"Samba, you did it!" I exclaimed, accidentally waking up my sisters.

"What is it? What are you doing?" one asked sleepily.

"It's Samba. He can read my mind!"

"That's crazy. Be quiet and go back to sleep," she murmured.

I looked over at Samba and thought I saw him wink.

"Okay," I agreed. "This will be our secret."

I drifted off to sleep that night, dreaming of shiny black eyes full of intelligence and possibilities yet to be discovered. Little did I know, this dream would resurface three decades later, and I would leave many things behind to follow it.

3

Hank Meets His Match

*The biggest adventure you can take is to live the life of
your dreams.*

Oprah Winfrey

JULY 2000

Tick. Tick. Tick. The clock on my office wall reminded me that
my life might be slipping away, one second at a time. My doctor's voice echoed in my mind . . .

"Mo," she said. "I need to prepare you for the worst-case
scenario."

"What do you mean?" I asked as my heart began to race.

"If the biopsy confirms ovarian cancer, as I suspect, you
may not have much time."

Stunned, I finally managed to ask, "How long?"

She paused and then replied, "Perhaps six months, but we'll
need to wait for the results and take it from there."

I listened to the clock tick as my thoughts returned to the present, and I tried to clear my foggy brain. Six months. I repeated the words as my mind automatically did the math. Six months . . . 180 days . . . 4,320 hours.

It had been three days since my biopsy, and the doctor's office still hadn't called with the results. Soon they would be closing for the weekend. I couldn't possibly wait until Monday. Should I call Dr. Miller? I picked up the phone and started to dial when the other line rang. I recognized the number and eagerly picked it up.

"Hello?"

"Hi," said Will. "Have you heard from the doctor's office yet?"

"No, not yet."

"Please don't worry; I'm sure everything will be fine." As always, the reassuring sound of Will's voice calmed my anxious thoughts. "Let's do something fun this weekend to take your mind off things. In fact, why don't I come pick you up at work? Can you be ready in an hour? I'll pack your bag."

"That's a great idea. I'll meet you out front."

I hung up the phone and looked at the growing stack of tax returns on my desk. As a CPA, I always found comfort in numbers. They helped me make sense of the world, the assurance that everything could be quantified. Now, nothing made sense.

Tick. Tick. Tick. I'd stared at that clock so often, surprised at how slowly time seemed to pass. Suddenly, time seemed to be going much too quickly. My life was getting shorter with each tick of the clock while I sat under fluorescent lights, preparing corporate tax returns. This was not the career I had dreamed about as a child. Will was right; time out in nature would help.

I slipped out the side door, not wanting to bump into any of my colleagues or clients. I decided to pop into the corner coffee shop for a cup of tea. I could use a boost of energy after my sleepless night.

I waited at the corner and my heart lifted when I saw Will's smiling face as his truck pulled up to the curb. I laughed at our two-year-old yellow lab, Bart, who was leaning out the window to greet me, ears flapping in the wind. Will reached out to help me and gave me a kiss as I piled into the front seat, juggling my briefcase, purse, and tea. I noticed there was camping gear in the back of the truck.

"Where are we going?" I kicked off my work shoes and tucked my legs beneath me, petting Bart as he settled in between us.

"We're going camping at the Seven Sacred Pools," Will replied with a grin. "I wanted to surprise you."

This certainly was a surprise since Will was usually the planner and I was the spontaneous one. Somehow, he always seemed to know exactly what I needed. The campground was just past the town of Hana, where we had spent our honeymoon twelve years before. It was one of our favorite places in the world. I clicked my seat belt into place and turned up the music as we drove the long and winding road to Hana.

Early the next morning, red cardinals chirped high overhead as I peeked my head out of the tent and breathed in the sweet, tropical air. I lifted the flap and stepped out, running my fingers through my hair. Will was already up and kneeling over the camp stove. Bart was sitting next to him, closely supervising the breakfast operation.

"Happy birthday!" Will said as he held out a stack of banana pancakes. Even though I was celebrating my thirty-ninth year, a single birthday candle danced in the light morning breeze.

I walked over to him with tears in my eyes. With everything that had been going on, I had forgotten it was my birthday.

"Make a wish," he said with a smile. I thought about all my birthday wishes when I was little and how I had always asked for the same thing. But this year and this wish were different.

I closed my eyes tightly and lifted up a silent prayer. *I wish for a second chance.*

I blew out the candle with one easy breath. Breathing in deeply, I looked up at the clear blue sky. The morning sun peeked through a canopy of green and warmed my face. I was eager to start our walk up to the waterfall.

The Waimoku Falls hike was our favorite one on Maui. It had a narrow trail that wound next to a slow river, zigzagging up through a bamboo forest until it reached a beautiful waterfall and swimming hole at the top. I hoped that being surrounded by nature with my two favorite people (well technically, one person and one dog) might help me to focus on the moment rather than the fact that I might have cancer.

We started out on the hike after breakfast and Will walked ahead of me, giving me time and space. It felt liberating to be out of the office and surrounded by nature. Bart walked in step beside me, staying even closer than usual.

"Will," I called out breathlessly after a mile or so. "I'm going to rest for a moment."

"Are you okay?" he asked, turning around with a look of concern.

"I just need some time to think," I replied.

"Well, if you're sure," he said, not sounding convinced.

"I'm fine," I said with a smile. "I'll catch up with you soon."

"Okay, keep Bart with you, and I'll see you at the top."

Will turned and headed up the trail, and I watched his strong athletic frame navigate the path effortlessly. Even after all this time, my handsome husband still made my heart skip a beat. His easy smile, keen intellect, and sky-blue eyes never failed to fill me with joy. I thought about what a gift it would be to grow old with this man and then remembered I might not have the chance.

I sighed and sat down on a log next to the river, slipping my backpack to the ground. I ran my hands across the moss that covered one side of the log, feeling every soft bump and ridge. Bart stared at me hopefully, wagging his tail. I picked up a stick and tossed it in the river for him. I'd had a special connection with Bart since he was a puppy. We attended an obedience class just for fun, but Bart was so smart that he went on to win state competitions. We competed at the highest level, where handlers are not allowed to use any words to communicate with their dogs, only hand signals. With Bart, even the hand signals weren't always necessary, as he often seemed to know what I wanted just from a look.

Bart held the stick in his mouth and playfully lowered his chest to the ground as he wagged his tail, his signal for *Let's play!* When he realized I wasn't in the mood, he wandered off to explore all the fascinating smells of the tropical rain forest.

I glanced at my watch and resisted the urge to mentally calculate how much of my "six months" had already slipped away. After all, I didn't know for sure I had cancer. But what if I did? I was surprised to discover that I didn't fear death as much as I felt a profound regret that I hadn't yet fulfilled my life's purpose. Watching Bart, my eyes filled with tears at the thought of how I might never see my childhood dream come true. I had always believed there was plenty of time. I remembered our pastor's message the previous week: how all of our talents, abilities, and passions are God's gift to us, and what we do with them is our gift back to him.

Looking down at my reflection in the river, I thought about all the time I had wasted letting fear stand in the way of my dreams. I'd struggled with anxiety most of my life, and now here I was, suddenly face-to-face with my biggest fear of all. I didn't want to die, but I also didn't want to waste any more precious time worrying. A simple prayer formed in my heart.

"Please, God, don't let this be cancer," I whispered as tears spilled down my cheeks. "Help me not to think about hospitals or surgery or anything else today. I just want to live in the moment and feel your presence."

The wind picked up and softly blew through my hair, caressing my face and bare arms.

The anxiety that had been squeezing my chest all morning began to dissolve. I closed my eyes. I breathed in the smell of strawberry guavas and noticed the songbirds singing sweetly in the trees overhead. I opened my eyes and saw Bart had returned from his adventures in the jungle. I patted my hand on the log and he hopped up and sat beside me.

"Thank you for this day, Lord. Thank you for Will and Bart and for this beautiful place. You've blessed me with so much."

Bart licked the salty tears from my cheek. As I looked at our reflection in the water, the wind subsided, and I saw our images clearly. A new thought sparked, and I felt a thrill of hope rise within me.

"And God," I added. "If you let me live, I promise to change what I'm doing with my life. I will dedicate the rest of my time to helping those in need and find the courage to follow the dreams that you put in my heart when I was a little girl. You know the ones."

As soon as I finished speaking those words, the fear faded away, and in its place, peace like a river flowed into my soul. I can only describe that heavenly peace as the complete reassurance that God had heard my prayer. I knew that no matter what happened next, I didn't want to waste another moment of my life. I stood up, grabbed my backpack, and walked quickly up the trail to catch up with Will. Bart ran alongside me, proudly carrying his new favorite stick.

When Bart and I reached the end of the trail, Will was waving from the top of the waterfall. I smiled and waved back as he dove into the sparkling pool of water below. Bart, who considered himself our private lifeguard, immediately charged into the water to rescue him while I peeled down to my swimsuit and jumped in after him.

Our laughter filled the air as the three of us swam behind the waterfall, where the air was much cooler. As we looked out through the falling water, the sun peeked from behind a cloud, and a brilliant rainbow stretched across the sky. My spirit soared as I stared in awe at the symbol of God's promise and knew in my heart that he would be with me no matter what came next.

Our trip to Hana had distracted me from worrying about my biopsy results. However, once we returned to civilization and Monday morning arrived, I found it difficult to set aside my fears. I sat at my desk, sipping a cup of tea. I was staring at the phone when it finally rang. My heart thudded in my chest as I answered and heard my doctor's voice.

"Mo, this is Dr. Miller," she said. "We've gotten the biopsy results back." I gripped the phone and held my breath. "I have good news," she said. I only heard bits and pieces of what came next: ". . . negative results . . . scheduling surgery . . . benign tumor." I thanked her and called Will with the good news that our prayers had been answered!

That day, I began to make plans for a radical change. As soon as I recovered from the surgery, I sold my CPA practice and enrolled at the Assistance Dog Institute in California. I was finally going to pursue my dream of training dogs to assist people with disabilities. Will took leave from his engineering job in order to support me in my new endeavor.

We looked online and found a small cottage to rent near Santa Rosa that was surrounded by towering redwood trees and only twenty minutes away from the school. Never one to sit idle, Will found a full-time job building an art studio. I tried not to think too much about being thirty-nine years old and having new college classmates who would probably be half my age. Instead, I focused on how thankful I was for a second chance. We left Bart with friends, packed our bags, and boarded a plane for California.

I looked out the window of the airplane and caught glimpses of the Pacific Ocean through billowy white clouds below. Will sat next to me, flipping through the in-flight magazine. I pressed my cheek against the window and felt the warmth of the sun. I thought about leaving my high-paying job as a CPA to become a dog trainer and heard the voices of those who had already expressed doubts about my decision. Negative what-if thoughts began to creep in. *What if I don't have what it takes to turn my dreams into reality? What if I have an anxiety attack in the middle of class? What if no one donates to the nonprofit and we go broke?* My heart started racing, but then I remembered how God had faithfully answered my prayers and given me new purpose. I looked at Will and thought about how blessed I was to have such a wonderful husband. I loved him with all my heart and felt that together we could accomplish anything.

Five hours later, I caught a glimpse of the stately Golden Gate Bridge stretching across the wide blue water far below. The sprawling city of San Francisco gleamed in the setting sun as our plane turned its nose and headed for a runway that looked like it was floating on water. I was filled with excitement about our new adventure as the plane touched down. We grabbed our luggage and took a shuttle to the rental car office and then drove north toward Santa Rosa.

The next morning we drove to the Assistance Dog Institute. It was located just outside of town and was surrounded by wineries and rolling hills. We passed rows of perfectly spaced grapevines with fat bunches of purple grapes sagging from the tangled tendrils that draped between posts. Will turned down a long gravel driveway and pulled into a parking lot next to an old beige building that used to house a juvenile detention center.

It was my first day of school and the first step toward my new life and mission! As I kissed Will goodbye and stepped out of the car, I was greeted by a cacophony of enthusiastic barking that came from a row of kennels near the entrance. They were filled with beautiful Labrador and golden retrievers. It looked like puppy heaven and I was drawn like a moth to a flame.

"Hold on," Will called out the window. "Don't forget your backpack!"

"Thanks," I said as I grabbed my backpack from his outstretched arm.

"Good luck," he called after me as I hurried toward the office. "And have fun!"

As I opened the door, I suddenly felt like a child attending my first day of school. I nervously glanced around, not certain where I should go next. An attractive woman with salt-and-pepper hair and bright blue eyes walked toward me with a big smile.

"Welcome to the Assistance Dog Institute," she said warmly.

"Thank you," I replied. "I'm so happy to be here."

I could hardly wait to get started. I joined the other students as we filed into our first lecture. I looked around and was relieved to discover I wasn't the oldest one in the class after all. Our instructor began with the course overview and described the various ways dogs can be trained to help people in need. I hung on her every word in spellbound fascination. By the end of the first hour, I knew I had made the right decision to give up my briefcase and calculator for leashes and dog treats.

Each student was assigned five dogs we were responsible for training, ranging from four-week-old puppies to two-year-old dogs. Instructors taught us how to use positive reinforcement to shape the puppies' behavior. We learned about canine cognition and how to encourage the dogs to problem solve and think for themselves. Although the days were long and the schedule demanding, I had never felt so energized in my life. I woke up each morning filled with a sense of purpose and excited to start the day. I was learning to train dogs to help people. My childhood dream was finally coming true!

I was astonished by how quickly my four-week-old puppy learned new things. His name was Oscar, and on the first day I taught him to "sit," "shake," and "come here." Our instructor explained the importance of early learning and how it creates additional neural pathways in dogs' brains. This helps them to perform more complicated skills later in life.

The oldest dogs were called "graduate dogs" and were getting ready to be matched with someone with a disability. They would then attend a two-week team training camp with their new partners before graduating. But first, each of us students was going to be paired with a graduate dog and attend a mock team training camp together. The instructors observed as we took turns interacting with the graduate dogs and matched us based on our personalities and interactions. It was like a canine form of speed dating, and from the beginning I only had eyes for Hank. He was a reddish golden retriever who was eager to please and always had a mischievous twinkle in his dark brown eyes. I think I speak for both of us when I say it was love at first sight.

There was a scientific method for pairing dogs and people based on the Wilson Learning Social Styles that many companies use for hiring employees. Several people who knew the dogs and the students completed a questionnaire that assessed each one's assertiveness and responsiveness levels. The social styles fell into four quadrants: analytical, driver, amiable, and expressive. The results were plotted on a chart that helped determine the best matches. I was initially skeptical about this method but saw how well it worked throughout the class. Most of the assistance dogs fell into the amiable category: less assertive but highly responsive. At the end of the first week the pairings were announced and I was thrilled to be partnered with Hank. We were both considered amiable-expressives, which meant we were fairly assertive and very responsive.

I spent the next month working from a wheelchair while teaching Hank advanced commands, like retrieving items and turning lights on and off. He also learned how to open doors. He was supposed to do this only when asked, but instead

Hank applied his newfound knowledge to open the latch on his kennel door *and* all the doors in the building in his attempts to find me wherever I was on campus.

I would often be sitting in a lecture, and Hank would pull open the door and come bounding into the room and run up to me with a wagging tail and triumphant smile. Much to his delight, everyone in the class laughed at his antics. Like many dogs, Hank was a comedian at heart.

The team training camp with the actual clients was scheduled to start the following week. I learned that Hank had been matched with a woman named Casey, who had limited mobility. She was a teacher at a community college in Santa Cruz, and her social style report was very similar to mine and Hank's. I read Casey's file and learned more about her so I could further specialize Hank's training. I was excited by the prospect of teaching Hank specific skills that would help Casey to become even more independent.

I was so excited to meet Casey that Will and I drove to Santa Cruz over the weekend to see where she worked and where Hank would be living. Feeling a little bit like a stalker, I slid down in the passenger seat as we drove past her house.

Casey's application described that when she was thirty-six years old, she had a stroke that affected her speech and caused paralysis on the right side of her body. She lived alone and wanted a service dog to help her both at home and at school. She used a power wheelchair for long distances but wanted a dog who could help her balance when she walked short distances. She also wanted a dog who would assist her with opening doors, carrying items, and turning lights on and off.

Casey especially needed help going up and down stairs. Hank learned to wear a customized leather harness that Casey

Casey and Service Dog Hank

could hold on to for balance and lean on if she needed help standing up. I was determined to get this part of Hank's training exactly right. The responsibility weighed heavily on me, knowing that if Hank ever took a wrong step, Casey could fall and be seriously injured.

Monday morning Casey arrived on campus with the other clients, and she and Hank hit it off immediately. Seeing them working together made my heart soar. The new teams attended alternating lectures and practice sessions throughout the day that were conducted by the students.

I was so proud watching Hank flawlessly perform all the skills I had taught him. During the first week, he kept looking over at me, but I had been instructed to ignore him—which was not easy to do! By the second week, Hank was completely focused on Casey. He was an intuitive dog and somehow seemed to understand that she needed his assistance, while I had been pretending.

Will and I spent a lot of time with Casey and enjoyed getting to know her. We appreciated her transparency and lack of pretense. She explained that because of her stroke, she had difficulty controlling her emotions. She laughed and cried easily and sometimes couldn't stop once she got started. Casey's laughter was infectious, and sometimes the three of us laughed so hard we cried. Hank got excited when this happened and did his helicopter tail-wag, which made us laugh even more!

A week before graduation, the school director visited our class and said she had an exciting announcement to make.

"Students, I have the most wonderful news. *The Oprah Show* is coming to film our graduation ceremony! Each of you will be filmed when you go onstage to introduce the dog you have trained and their new partner."

As my classmates cheered and talked excitedly, I sat quietly in disbelief. I was filled with dread at the thought of speaking in front of not just a large crowd but also television cameras for a program that would be broadcast to millions. After a sleepless night, I met with my instructor the next day at her office.

"I'm so sorry, but I just can't do it," I said as I sat across the desk from her.

"I understand your fear of public speaking, but this is a necessary skill for you to have," she replied. I squirmed in my seat. "I'm afraid you won't be able to graduate unless you speak at the ceremony."

When the big day arrived, I stood backstage, peeking out from behind a heavy curtain as my classmates were called onstage one at a time to present the dogs they trained to their new partners. *The Oprah Show*'s crew was in the front row, with huge cameras and lights pointed at the stage. Thankfully, Oprah was not there, or I might have fainted on the spot.

Will knew how terrified I was and gave me a big smile and a thumbs-up from where he and Casey were sitting. Earlier, she had asked Will if he would help her walk onto the stage, as she didn't want to use her wheelchair. Seeing the two of them helped give me the courage to approach the podium with Hank when my name was finally called.

As I stood at the podium, I wondered if it was physically possible for my heart to pound right out of my chest. My mouth was dry, and my tongue was stuck to its roof. In one hand were my note cards, and in the other was Hank's leash. Both were shaking. Hank stood by my side, smiling at the audience. I somehow managed to squeak out the words on my note cards.

When I introduced Casey as Hank's new partner, Will gallantly offered her his arm and they took one careful step at a time toward the center of the stage. I walked toward them with Hank and handed his leash over to Casey and gave her a hug.

"Thank you, Mo," she whispered, with tears running down her face. "You have no idea how much Hank means to me. He is the best gift ever."

At that moment, I forgot all about the cameras and everyone else in the room.

We returned to Maui inspired by Casey and Hank's partnership and more excited than ever to start an assistance dog program.

The best part was that Will was just as enthusiastic about our new mission as I was. He is a huge dog lover, but more importantly, he has a servant's heart and truly loves helping people in need. I could not have asked for a better partner in this new endeavor.

The day we returned home, Will made a desk for me out of an old door he found in the garage. He set it up in the corner of our small living room and I placed all the books I'd brought back from school on it. I had my first office—well, technically just a desk, but still! My mind was bursting with all my newly acquired knowledge about training assistance dogs.

I wanted to create a program that would not only help people reach their full potential but also bring out the best in the dogs. My plan was to keep the program small and train one or two dogs at a time from our home. I wanted to create partnerships that were based on mutual love, trust, and respect. It was important to ensure the dogs' emotional and physical needs were met before they were asked to help someone else. Only positive training methods would be used so the dogs would enjoy learning. I wanted to make sure that each dog was carefully matched with their partner—so they loved what they did and who they did it for.

Bart lay at my feet as I thought about where to start. I made a list of all the things I needed to do to launch a nonprofit organization. Although I had a business degree, running a nonprofit was not my area of expertise, so I bought a few books on the subject. I learned that one of the first things to do was to create policies and rules for the new organization. This sounded like a good idea, so I took a stab at it.

The first draft of the Assistance Dogs of Hawaii (ADH) policies and rules included:

Rule #1: Start with purpose-bred dogs.

Rule #2: Carefully match dogs with their partners.

Rule #3: Charge an appropriate fee.

Rule #4: Train Labrador and golden retrievers.

Rule #5: Get a physician's referral.

Rule #6: Train service dogs to assist those with limited mobility.

Rule #7: Minimum age requirement is ten years old.

Rule #8: Begin training at eight weeks old.

Rule #9: Place dogs only in Hawaii.

I like round numbers, so it couldn't possibly end on #9. I tried to think of one more. This one was outside the box, but I tend to overempathize at times, so I decided to include

Rule #10: Don't ever cry in front of clients.

The next morning, I checked my messages and the first one was from a woman named Feanna, who lived on Maui. She had a spinal cord injury and wanted to apply for a service dog to help her with physical tasks.

"Well," I said to myself, "this sounds like a pretty good place to start."

Little did I know I was about to meet someone so inspiring she would change my perspective on life forever.

4

A Knight
in Shining Armor

*Although the world is full of suffering, it is also full of
the overcoming of it.*

Helen Keller

The next morning, I called Feanna and we went through the
interview questionnaire for new applicants. She explained that
when she was fifteen years old, she'd gone swimming with
her friends at a lake. They were playing on a rope swing and
jumping into the water. When it was Feanna's turn, the branch
holding the rope broke and she fell into the shallow water. Her
neck was broken, and she was instantly paralyzed. Her injury
was at the C4–C5 level at the top part of the spine. Because of
the location, she was paralyzed from the neck down and had
severe damage to her central nervous system.

Despite her many challenges, Feanna had a great attitude and sounded like an ideal candidate for a service dog. That is, until she dropped the bomb.

"I heard you were starting the program and got so excited, I just couldn't wait. I found the best puppy for you to train," she said. "I can't wait for you to meet him!"

"Oh, Feanna, I'm sorry," I replied. "We're only going to be training purpose-bred retrievers since they have the best chance of making it through all the necessary health and temperament screenings."

"You don't have to worry about that," she responded brightly. "He is a Labrador and comes from very good lines. His grandfather was a champion."

"That's wonderful," I said. "But the puppies need to go through our training program before we match them with someone. There are so many factors that go into making a successful match, like personality, environment, and energy level."

"I'm certain Knight is the perfect match for me," she said, undaunted. "I can't wait for you to meet him and see for yourself."

I smiled, knowing when I was beaten, and we scheduled an appointment for the next day. I had to admire Feanna's optimism and was looking forward to meeting her. I'd simply explain our program's policies and that we'd be happy to eventually match a fully trained dog with her.

I've always had a hard time saying no, so I rehearsed my speech on the drive over and was prepared to stand firm. Feanna lived in Maui Meadows, a neighborhood of lovely homes on a hillside above the beach. At the top of her driveway was a big lawn, surrounded by a dense hibiscus hedge.

I looked over the hedge to the whitecapped ocean and took a deep breath as I approached the front door and knocked.

A young boy opened the door and welcomed me into their home. He led me to the living room where a lovely woman with wavy brown hair sat in a power wheelchair next to an easel that had a painting in progress. There was a black Labrador puppy lying at her feet. He was a beautiful representation of the breed, with his barrel chest, broad head, and intelligent expression.

"Welcome! You must be Mo." Her smile was radiant, as if she had an inner light. "I'm Feanna and I'm so thrilled you're here." Her voice had a musical quality to it, and I was instantly captivated by her bright spirit.

"Thanks for inviting me. It's a pleasure to meet you."

"This is my son, Kaisho, and my puppy, Knight."

Kaisho held out his hand in greeting and bowed his head in the Japanese custom.

"Hi, Kaisho. It's nice to meet you," I said as I shook his hand and bowed my head in return. I leaned down to say hello to Knight and was surprised when he lifted a paw and shook my hand too. He had a noble expression, and I was impressed by his calm demeanor.

I asked Feanna about the painting she was working on. It was a whimsical underwater scene with brightly colored fish that looked as cheerful as she was. Feanna wore a brace on her left hand that had an attachment for a paintbrush. She explained she was not able to make brush strokes and proceeded to show me how she painted. With tremendous effort, she moved her elbow and shoulder to position the tip of the brush in front of the canvas. She carefully made one dot, and her entire face lit up with a look of accomplishment.

Despite being paralyzed from the neck down, Feanna had clearly discovered the secret of happiness and found delight in the smallest things. She had named the painting "Underwater Dance," and her joy shone through in each one of the thousands of brightly colored dots.

"I love snorkeling and wanted to share the freedom I feel and all the beauty I see underwater. I've been working on it for months and am almost finished," she beamed.

"It's beautiful," I said, mesmerized by the dance of the colorful tropical fish.

We all went outside and sat together on her lanai. "Kaisho, will you please bring out the iced tea?" she asked. He brought a tray of drinks and placed it on the table. I watched as he held the glass up for his mother and positioned the straw at her lips so she could take a drink. Watching them together, I could feel the love they shared. When she finished drinking, Kaisho went back inside and Knight trotted across the lawn to the hibiscus hedge. I watched in amazement as he picked a bright yellow hibiscus flower and walked back to Feanna carrying it in his mouth. He jumped up and placed his paws on her lap. Even with her limited movement, she was able to take the flower from him.

"Thank you, Knight," she said with a smile.

"Knight knows how much I love flowers," she explained. "He picks one for me every day."

I noted Knight had a strong retrieve instinct and was incredibly handler-focused—two important traits for a service dog.

"How did he get his name?" I asked.

"I knew the first time I saw him that he was going to be my knight in shining armor."

Feanna and Service Dog Knight

I reminded myself that dogs in our program needed to be carefully matched with their partners *after* they completed all their training and health and temperament screenings. But I could already feel my resolve weakening.

Feanna shared the story of her life with me that afternoon. Soon after her accident, her father's job required their family to move from California to Japan. She attended high school there and quickly became immersed in the Japanese culture.

When she'd been there several years, Feanna took an art class and met a young artist named Koichi. He and Feanna soon discovered they were kindred spirits and eventually fell in love and got married. Doctors advised them she would not be able to have children, but they had a son and daughter, Kaisho and Aquanna. Doctors also said Feanna could not have natural childbirth, but she accomplished that too.

Together, Feanna and Koichi experienced many other things no one thought possible. Koichi loved Feanna's adventurous spirit and was determined that she would enjoy life to the fullest. Together, they climbed mountains, sailed, and even went scuba diving. They both became successful artists and traveled the country, exhibiting their art. Their dream had always been to live in Hawaii, and they had been on Maui less than a year when I met them.

When I asked Feanna why she wanted a service dog, it came back to her art. One afternoon she had been home alone and working on a painting. She dropped her paintbrush and felt frustrated because she couldn't pick it up and continue painting. The afternoon slowly wore on and it began to get dark. As she sat all alone in the darkening room, she imagined having a service dog who could turn on the light and pick up her paintbrush for her. This experience was a turning point for her. She was determined never to feel so helpless again.

Her story tugged at my heart and I wanted more than anything to help her. Despite her challenges, she didn't see herself as a victim. She had already overcome so many obstacles in her life and I wanted to help her accomplish even more. Being in Feanna's presence was like being in a love bubble. It felt as if there was an invisible field around her that people were pulled into if they got close enough, and I was already beginning to feel the pull.

Just before I left, Feanna asked about the cost of training a service dog. At school, we had been advised to charge a reasonable fee for the dogs, since there are significant costs involved in the training and lifetime follow-up support. When I told her what it would cost, her eyes filled with tears.

"There's no way we can afford that," she replied. "Money has been tight since we moved here, and we're barely making ends meet."

An hour later, I was driving home with Knight sitting next to me in the passenger seat. I stared at the road ahead and thought about all the rules I had already broken on my first day on the job:

~~Rule #1: Start with purpose-bred dogs.~~

~~Rule #2: Carefully match dogs with their partners.~~

(And, last but not least . . .)

~~Rule #3: Charge an appropriate fee.~~

What was I thinking? Had I been hypnotized? Then I looked over at Knight in the passenger seat and knew it was the right decision. I had my first official student and could never have asked for a better pupil.

Will and Bart shared a look of surprise when I walked through the door with our new family member that evening. Within minutes, they fell in love with Knight too. I explained that he was going to live with us for a year while he went through the training program. Knight followed Bart everywhere, and each time I taught Knight a new skill, Bart was happy to demonstrate how it was done.

Knight quickly progressed through the curriculum for the four different stages of training: kindergarten puppy training (2–6 months old), basic training (7–12 months old), advanced training (13–17 months old), and graduate training (18 months old +). I encouraged him to think and problem solve from an early age, using interactive puzzles and games to build his self-confidence. This would help him to not give up when he encountered challenges later in life.

Knight went everywhere with us: to stores, church, restaurants, movie theaters, and the beach. He seemed like an old dog in a puppy body and rarely made a mistake. Knight was unflappable. The only time I ever saw him startle was once at the shopping mall. We were walking past Macy's and there was a naked and headless mannequin in the display window. Knight stopped dead in his tracks and did a double take. His eyes widened as he took a step backward and cocked his head with a look of concern. I recognized this as a teachable moment and decided to take him inside the store for a closer look. I was eager to apply what I had learned in school about counterconditioning and replacing a negative association with a positive one.

Giving Knight plenty of space, I slowly approached the mannequin to show him that it wasn't real. But as I smiled reassuringly and reached out to touch it, its arm fell off in my hand! I glanced over at Knight, who was trying his best to keep his composure, despite the headless and now armless person in front of him. Eventually, with plenty of treats, he cautiously approached what was left of the body and appeared quite relieved to discover it wasn't a real person.

Knight soon mastered everything in the kindergarten and basic training classes. These included standard obedience cues like "sit," "stay," and "heel." (I like to use the word *cue* instead of *command* since we encourage rather than force a behavior.) Other cues were specific for assistance dogs, like "push," to touch an item with his paw. This would eventually be used to push buttons to open doors or to push a button for emergency response.

During this time, I spent long hours establishing the non-profit organization and training Knight, but it never felt like work because I was enjoying every minute. By the time he was ten months old, Knight progressed to the advanced training class and learned skills such as tugging open a door, turning on and off lights, and retrieving objects.

We practiced in public places so Knight could learn to ignore environmental distractions, one of the most important requirements for a service dog. Distractions vary for each dog and include everything from smells on the ground to food, people, cats, dogs, birds, or children playing catch with a ball. Knight was excellent at ignoring other animals and people when we were training. The biggest challenge for Knight was food. Like most Labradors, Knight was a foodie. Although we never gave him people food, he was an optimist and always remained hopeful.

We often practiced "leave it," the cue to walk by food on the ground or ignore food being handed to him by strangers. One day, we were practicing at home with a peanut butter cookie placed in the middle of our living room floor. I was pleased to see that he finally seemed to have grasped the importance of this exercise and was showing some self-restraint. You would have thought the cookie was poison by the way Knight made a huge detour around it. Each time we walked by, he dramatically turned his head away and refused to even look at it!

"Good boy, Knight. You're really getting it, aren't you?" I praised him just as the doorbell rang. I signed for a FedEx delivery and returned to our training session a moment later. Knight sat in the middle of the room, avoiding my gaze. He was the picture of abject guilt. The cookie had disappeared . . . except for the telltale sign of crumbs on his chin.

Despite some early setbacks, Knight's conduct was soon impeccable. Once he mastered the ninety standard assistance dog cues, he entered graduate training and began learning specialized skills to assist Feanna. I couldn't bear the thought of her having to wait for help if she dropped her paintbrush again, so Knight learned to pick it up by the wooden handle and deliver it to my hand. Since Feanna's motorized wheelchair couldn't operate if there were objects in its path, he also learned to pick up items off the floor and drop them into a basket.

To aid in Knight's training, we purchased a used wheelchair. And not just any wheelchair—it was a giant one! I looked pretty silly driving it, as it was three times my size. It took some practice before I learned to maneuver the big rig without banging into any walls. Knight and I went to places Feanna was planning to go to, like Safeway and Home Depot, so he could get used to heeling next to a wheelchair in those environments.

We often encountered people I knew, who looked alarmed at seeing me in a wheelchair and were not sure what to say.

"I'm fine. We're just training!" I'd say with a smile as we cruised by.

One of Feanna's biggest goals was to go to the store by herself without having to ask anyone for help. I taught Knight a sequence of cues to unzip Feanna's backpack, remove her wallet, and give it to the cashier.

I started by asking, "Knight, will you help me?"

His expression and body language always gave the same answer: *Yes, of course I will!*

Then I said, "Get the wallet," and he'd walk behind the wheelchair to where the backpack hung.

"Tug," I said. He'd grab the little strap on the backpack's zipper and carefully unzip it with his teeth.

"Get it," I encouraged, and he'd stick his head in the backpack and proudly emerge with the wallet in his mouth.

"Hold," I said, and followed it with "up." Once his paws were up on the counter, I said, "Drop it," and he'd lean forward and drop the wallet on the counter.

Feanna also wanted him to get specific items off the shelves in the store and place them on her wheelchair tray, which was directly above her lap. This involved teaching Knight another sequence of cues that I hadn't seen used before but was sure he could learn. To help with this, Will installed shelves in our garage and placed different objects on them. He also attached a tray like Feanna's to my wheelchair.

"Look," was Knight's cue to search for an item. He also learned to "look up," "look down," "look left," and "look right." When Knight's eyes were on the correct object, I said, "That's it," followed by "get it" and "bring it here." Next, I said, "Step," and he placed his front feet on my wheelchair footrest, and finally, "Drop it," and he dropped the item on my tray.

After a year of training, Knight had become an exemplary service dog, and I was so proud of him. Feanna attended a two-week team training camp with him, where they learned to work together as a team. We celebrated their accomplishment with a small graduation ceremony, and he moved back home with Feanna, who was delighted to be reunited with him.

A few days later, Feanna ventured out with Knight for the first time. She wheeled about a mile to a small convenience store by the beach. Shoppers watched in amazement as Knight got the items she asked for off the shelves and placed them on her tray. Feanna wheeled up to the counter and said, "Get the wallet," and Knight unzipped the backpack hanging on the back of her wheelchair, carefully took out the wallet, placed his paws on the counter, and gave the wallet to the astounded cashier.

Feanna was feeling triumphant on her way home from the store, until the handle she used to control her wheelchair fell off and rolled underneath it. She was stranded on the side of the busy road, which had always been her biggest fear. After a moment's panic, she noticed Knight was looking expectantly up at her, ready to help.

"Knight, will you help me?" she asked. He wagged his tail in an affirmative reply. "Look," she said, as she gestured toward the ground. He searched until he located the handle under her wheelchair. "That's it," she encouraged. "Get it." He tried to reach it with his mouth, but it was too far. He solved the problem by lying on his side on the asphalt and reaching with his paw until he eventually dragged the handle out from under the chair. He carefully picked it up with his mouth, stepped onto her footrest, and placed it on her tray. She was able to use her wrists to reattach it to the joystick, and they safely continued their journey home.

A month after they graduated, I was at Feanna's house for their first follow-up visit. We sat outside as the warm trade winds ruffled the umbrella that shaded us from the midday sun. I held her glass of mango iced tea and placed the straw to her lips. She took a long drink and nodded her head to let me know she was finished.

"I've been meaning to thank you for teaching Knight to straighten out my hands."

"What do you mean?" I asked.

"Each morning, the first thing he does when we wake up is to stand over me and stare into my eyes," she explained. "Then, he places a paw on my forearm to hold it still and licks my hand to uncurl my fingers. Once they are straightened, he looks into my eyes and repeats the process with my other hand. I've started to get some movement back in my hands because of him." To my amazement, she uncurled her fingers partway.

"I never taught him to do that!" I said in surprise.

"I think he knows there is something wrong with my hands and is trying to fix them," she said with a smile.

This was the first of many times that I witnessed a graduate dog go above and beyond what they had been taught in order to help their partner.

The following week, I was scheduled to give a lunchtime presentation for the Rotary Club of Kihei. Public speaking was still a thorn in my side, so I invited Feanna to come with me for moral support and to talk about Knight. After I stuttered through a brief introduction to the crowd, she calmly wheeled onto the stage with Knight by her side. He lay down next to her wheelchair and gazed adoringly up at her as she began speaking.

"When you look at Knight, you probably just see a dog," she began. "But when I look at Knight, I see the past, present, and future. I see a past of sitting alone in the dark and helplessly waiting for someone to come home and turn on the light for me. When I look at Knight, I see a present that is filled with unconditional love and companionship." She smiled down at him and he wagged his tail as if on cue. "When I look at Knight, I see a future that is now filled with hope, independence, and endless possibilities." She went on to describe the many ways Knight had already changed her life. It was the most moving speech I'd ever heard.

Over the years, Feanna's independence continued to grow with Knight by her side. When Knight was five years old, Feanna and her family decided to move back to Japan. Before she left, I went to their house to say a final goodbye.

When I was getting ready to leave, she said, "Wait, I have a gift for you," and gestured toward a present on the coffee table. I sat on the sofa as she watched me unfold the delicate Japanese wrapping paper.

"Oh Feanna, I can't believe it. Thank you so much!"

It was the painting called "Underwater Dance" that she had been working on the first day we met. Feanna's painting would always remind me of her bright spirit and that we can always choose to be joyful in spite of our circumstances. I was sad to see Feanna go but grateful for all she had taught me.

Feanna wrote to me often, describing her life in Japan, and I continued to provide her with follow-up support. Her family lived in Kyoto, where she and Knight volunteered at a school for children with disabilities. She took Knight for walks each day along the Kamogawa River. The path was lined with cherry trees and in the springtime, Knight picked up the cherry blossoms and gave them to Feanna.

Knight was especially comforting to Feanna during her husband's long battle with cancer. When Koichi died, Knight became even more devoted to Feanna and never left her side. As he grew older, he began having difficulty jumping up onto her bed, so she had a ramp built for him. Even when he could no longer see, he continued to retrieve items that she dropped by scent alone.

Over the years, the walks along the river got shorter and the time he spent in bed got longer. Knight's eyesight and hearing were failing, but Feanna said their soul connection was stronger than ever.

During the winter when Knight was sixteen years old, Feanna knew that his time was getting close. She promised him that if he would just hold on until springtime, she would take him to the town's cherry blossom festival one last time. Knight somehow made it until April, and the family gathered and gently placed him in a wagon that Aquanna had lined with blankets. Kaisho pulled the wagon, and Feanna wheeled next to her Knight in Shining Armor. Friends and neighbors joined them as they made their way to the cherry blossom festival. Along the way, more and more people joined the procession to honor this faithful companion they had known and admired for so many years. Knight's face was white, and his eyes were clouded over, but he smiled peacefully as they went together through the tunnel of cherry trees. The wind whispered through the trees, and pink petals fell softly onto Knight's black coat as he and Feanna traveled the road one last time.

5

Leader Shows the Way

Start by doing what's necessary; then do what's possible; and suddenly you're doing the impossible.

Saint Francis of Assisi

My feet were still covered in sand from a day at the beach as I drove home on Mokulele Highway, a long stretch of road that runs across the middle of the island. Thousands of years ago, Maui was two separate islands—to the east was Haleakala Crater, a majestic ten-thousand-foot-tall shield volcano that the original settlers named the "house of the sun." To the west were the rugged and impassable West Maui Mountains.

A single building peeked out from a sea of sugarcane fields, and I felt a familiar urge to pull into the parking lot of the Humane Society. I liked to cheer up the homeless dogs that were there and often stopped to visit them and offer some words of encouragement. I pulled on my beach cover-up and ran my fingers through my salty, damp hair. As I approached the main entrance, I could hear barking coming from the kennels out back and tried to mentally prepare myself for what I was about to encounter. The dogs' eyes and body language always spoke volumes, and it broke my heart to see the ones who looked confused and scared. I focused on lifting their spirits and slipping them a biscuit or two. I waved at the receptionist, who looked up from a phone call, smiled, and mouthed, "Hi, Mo." I pointed toward the kennel area and she gave me a thumbs-up. I pushed open the heavy metal door and a cacophony of barking dogs bombarded my senses first. It was soon followed by the familiar pungent smell, which was made worse by the heat and humidity of the late afternoon.

The chain-link kennels were in two rows and I walked along the path in front of the doors, stopping to say hello to each dog. There were all types, ages, and sizes of dogs. Many were pit bull mixes and Chihuahua mixes, two of the most popular breeds on the island. Some didn't even lift their heads when I said hello. They just glanced up at me with a look of such defeat that I could tell they had given up hope. Others were happily oblivious to their plight and took a break from playing with their kennel mates to greet me through the fence.

In the very last kennel was a solitary puppy, who appeared to be about three months old. He was sitting patiently at the gate as if he had been waiting for me. He was a German shepherd mix with beautiful black and brown markings and ears that stood out at half-mast. I was struck by his calm and intelligent expression and had a feeling I was in the presence of an old soul. Rather than looking dejected or acting excited like the dogs surrounding him, he was completely composed and had an air of quiet dignity. His fathomless dark brown eyes looked directly at me and reached into my soul.

"Hello, brother," I said as I crouched down in front of the gate. He approached and sat directly in front of me, all the while keeping direct eye contact, which was unusual.

I reached my fingers through the chain link and rubbed his coarse fur between them. My eyes suddenly filled with tears as memories of the neglected German shepherd I had befriended as a child came flooding back. The puppy gently leaned against the fence and pressed his shoulder into my hand. I reached my fingers as far as I could to give his skinny little chest a scratch.

"You're such a good boy. How did you end up here?" I asked him.

He looked back at me and had no answer. I stood up and read the information sheet that was fastened to his kennel. It said he was a twelve-week-old shepherd mix and had been abandoned along with his littermates. And his birthday was July 28 . . . the same day as mine! This was obviously some sort of sign, and I suspected right then he was coming home with me.

"Don't worry; I'll be right back," I assured him. I went to the reception office and asked if they had any more information on puppy #107.

"I'm sorry; we don't really have much," the receptionist said. "It looks like the litter was found abandoned in a sugarcane field. Some workers saw them and notified us." She paused for a moment and then added, "He's been here for over three weeks, and we're at full capacity." The implication was not lost on me.

I asked for him to be brought to the exercise yard, where there was more room for potential adopters to interact with the dogs. When the attendant opened the gate to let the puppy in, I was surprised when he ignored all the smells on the ground and came right over and sat by me. We chatted for a while, and I told him about Will and our program and how he might be able to help someone in need one day. He listened politely as I rubbed his ears and gave him the last of the dog biscuits in my pocket.

A half hour later, I was completing the adoption paperwork at the front desk when they brought him out.

"He's a special one," the attendant said as he walked him around the tall counter and handed me his leash. The receptionist held the door open for us as I thanked them and said goodbye.

"Please call us when you choose a name, and we'll put it in his file," she said.

I looked down at the puppy walking by my side. "Oh, I already know his name," I said with a smile. "It's Leader."

Leader rode in the passenger seat, and on the way home, I watched him out of the corner of my eye. I wondered what he was thinking as he looked contemplatively out the window at the sugarcane fields passing by. I was thinking that I had just broken another rule:

Rule #4: ~~Train Labrador and golden retrievers.~~

Will and I had recently moved the office to a donated retail space at the Queen Ka'ahumanu Center. I was so thankful to finally have a dedicated space to teach Leader and his classmates. I was amazed by the outpouring of community support we received as more and more people learned about the program.

Leader was an excellent student and progressed easily through the first two stages of training. He stood out among his peers, who were all golden retrievers and Labradors. He was a tall dog with a beautiful brown-and-black coat and a white blaze on his chest. The markings around his almond-shaped eyes made him look like he was wearing glasses. This gave him a distinctly intellectual appearance. Leader's best friend was a spunky yellow Labrador named Chipper, who had been donated to our program by the guide dog school in New Zealand. Chipper was a month older than Leader, but Leader quickly grew into his large German shepherd frame. The two puppies were inseparable, except when Chipper was getting into trouble—then Leader would have no part of it. Despite his humble beginnings, he was always a gentleman and had a strict code of conduct.

One morning, I was at our new office and received a phone call from a woman named Marianne who lived on the island of Hawaii, also known as the Big Island. She wanted a service dog for her ten-year-old son, Martin. She explained that he had Duchenne muscular dystrophy, a progressive disease that causes severe muscle weakness and atrophy. Martin had been on a waiting list for a service dog from the mainland for a while, and during that time he continued to lose more mobility. They had heard about our program and were hoping that Martin might be able to get a dog before his disease progressed any further.

I didn't have the heart to tell her that we hadn't placed any dogs with children yet. Instead, I listened as she told me about Martin, who used a power wheelchair, was an excellent student, and sounded like a great candidate for a service dog. As she described her son and the type of assistance he needed, I looked at Leader and pictured him walking alongside Martin in his wheelchair on their way to school.

A month later, I was on my way to the Big Island to meet Martin and his family in the town of Hilo, where they lived. Their family was originally from Germany, and Martin's father worked at the observatory on the top of Mauna Kea. At 13,800 feet, it is the highest point in Hawaii and one of the clearest places on earth to observe the galaxies.

I booked a flight on a new interisland airline to save money. The plane was tiny, and the six inches of legroom in front of my seat were taken up with seventy-five pounds of German shepherd. I curled my legs underneath me and glanced around the plane. There were only three other passengers. The pilot, who was sitting directly in front of me, appeared to be about fifteen years old. It began to dawn on me that this might not have been the best idea.

We took off down the runway and ascended into the clouds. The plane started to bounce violently up and down, and I was thankful for Leader, who calmly rested his head on my lap. We left Maui behind and were crossing the Alenuihaha Channel toward the Big Island when the plane suddenly dropped about a hundred feet and everyone screamed.

I looked to the pilot for reassurance, but he was no longer there. Panicked, I leaned around his seat and saw him bent over the floor. For a horrifying moment, I thought he had passed out. I shook his arm and he quickly popped back up.

"Are you okay?" I asked.

"I'm fine. Just dropped something," he said with a smile.

I leaned back in my seat and made a mental note to travel only on major airlines in the future. I spent the remainder of the flight studying the control panel and watching how he flew the plane, just in case. Thankfully, for everyone on board, my services were not required.

We landed in Hilo, rented a car, and drove up to Martin's house. It was located on four acres in the rolling green hills above the city. Martin and his family were delightful and so thankful we had come all the way from Maui to see them. Martin's body was frail, but he had bright eyes and a very quick wit. Leader seemed fascinated by him as he zipped around the house in his small power wheelchair. When his father picked Martin up to carry him to the bathroom, Leader followed them down the hallway and waited outside the door. It occurred to me that Leader's breed made him particularly well suited to be placed with a child. German shepherds were bred to watch over the flock and have a strong caretaking instinct.

Martin's parents, Marianne and Klaus, were so positive and had a great can-do attitude. By the time Leader and I left that evening, I felt confident that Martin would be a good match for him. I could hardly wait to get back to Maui and start teaching Leader specialized skills to assist Martin.

The next day, I arrived at the office and found a note from the mall manager—they had tenants for the space we'd been using and needed us to move out. I was disheartened but soon found out they were donating an even bigger space just around the corner.

A week later, I sat at my desk in our new and improved office with a cup of steaming hot tea and reviewed Martin's application. I noticed that on the physician's referral form, the box requesting a phone consultation was marked yes. I called his doctor and was surprised when he said that he didn't think Martin was a good candidate for a service dog.

"Why not?" I asked in disbelief.

"The application states that service dogs are supposed to help increase their partner's independence," he replied. "I'm afraid that's not going to be the case with Martin. He is a dying child."

"What is his prognosis?" I asked with a feeling of dread.

"I estimate his life expectancy to be about sixteen years."

I hung up the phone and looked over at Leader. He'd noticed the tone of my voice and cocked his head toward me with a look of concern. I remembered what I'd been taught about placing the dogs where they'd be most helpful. Part of that meant considering the longevity of the placement. I chose to make a decision based on hope rather than fear.

Rule #5: Get a physician's referral.

Leader entered graduate training and learned specialized skills to assist Martin, such as picking up pieces of paper and pencils that often fell while Martin was doing schoolwork. I tried to simulate Martin's limited movement so the transition would be easier for Leader when he began working with him. Leader learned to place his long muzzle under my forearm when it was hanging at my side and carefully lift it back onto the wheelchair armrest. This would help Martin, who was having increasing difficulty moving his arms.

One important skill the family wanted Leader to learn was to wake up Klaus during the night when Martin needed help. Martin didn't have the voice capacity to call out loudly enough for his father to hear, even with the monitor they had placed on his nightstand. Will and I practiced at home. I lay on the couch in the living room and whispered, "Go find Dad," which

Martin and Service Dog Leader

was his cue. Leader ran into the bedroom where Will pretended to be asleep and nudged him with his nose to wake him up.

Marianne said that one reason Martin needed help at night was because he sometimes got too hot and didn't have the strength to pull the covers off.

"Perhaps I could teach Leader to pull the covers off for him so you wouldn't need to get up as often," I suggested.

"Do you really think he could learn to do that?" Marianne asked with excitement.

"I think so. I'll give it a try and let you know how it goes."

That evening I was sitting in bed next to Will, who was reading a book. I tried to be still and not bother him while I held out my corner of the blanket to Leader.

"Get it. Tug!" I whispered, and he gingerly took it in his mouth.

"That's it!" I encouraged as he hesitatingly pulled the corner back an inch or two. He knew how to tug open a heavy door but was clearly reluctant to pull the covers off. No one was more of a stickler than Leader on proper etiquette, and I could tell by his disapproving expression that he considered this a highly unusual request on my part.

His classmate Chipper was also living with us at the time. He woke up and looked excited when he heard the word *tug*.

"Okay, Chipper, would *you* like to give it a try?" I asked, while glancing at Leader with a meaningful look.

Chipper replied, *You bet I would!* with his eager smile and fast tail-wag.

I held out the corner of the blanket to him and whispered, "Tug."

Chipper grabbed it with gusto and backed up across the room until he pulled the blanket completely off the bed and onto the floor. Leader heard Will and me laughing at Chipper's extra effort and decided he would like another try after all. This type of rivalry training works well, since the dogs learn by observing each other and don't like to be upstaged by their classmates.

Soon, Leader mastered all the skills, including pulling the blanket down just the right amount. It was time for team training camp. Martin and Marianne arrived at the Kahului Airport, and Will picked them up in our newly acquired, but very old, wheelchair van.

Because of Martin's age, Marianne needed to attend the class with him and take all the written exams. These required a score of at least 90 percent to pass.

Martin was unusually quiet the first morning of class, and I asked him if everything was okay. He nodded, but Marianne shared that he was very nervous about the tests.

"Martin, I know you're an excellent student, and I have complete confidence in you," I reassured him. "Don't worry; you'll do great."

He looked at me with raised eyebrows and said, "Oh, it's not me I'm worried about. It's my mom. She hasn't been in school in a really long time. Will I still get Leader if she flunks the tests?" Thankfully, they were both outstanding students and completed the first week of training with flying colors.

For the second week of team training camp, Leader and I traveled with them back to Hilo. The first day, we practiced skills at their home, like opening doors and turning on lights. I watched proudly as Leader carefully pulled down the blanket for Martin—just the right amount. We practiced "Go find Dad" several times, knowing that Martin's life could one day depend on Leader correctly performing this skill.

The following day, we went to the shopping mall in Hilo. As soon as we were inside, Martin said, "Leader, let's go!" and they took off together, leaving Marianne and me in the dust. I was about to run after them, but Marianne stopped me.

"Let them go," she said with a smile. "This is the first time Martin has wanted to be on his own. It's wonderful to see him being so independent."

We followed them around the mall, and I was impressed by how perfectly Leader walked next to Martin's wheelchair and how confident they both looked. Martin had a bumper sticker on the back of his wheelchair that said, "Dog is my copilot." Leader was tall enough that his head was even with the armrest. Martin's tiny hand gently stroked Leader's ear as they traveled along. Each time Martin said, "Good dog," Leader smiled up at him, and his thick shepherd tail waved in response.

They approached Macy's department store and Martin wheeled up to the automatic door and said, "Leader, touch."

Shoppers stopped and watched in amazement as Leader touched the button with his nose and it slowly swung open.

"Go through," Martin said, and Leader obediently walked through the doorway and turned to face Martin.

"Back," he continued, and Leader slowly backed up as Martin moved forward.

When they were safely inside, Martin said, "Heel," and Leader returned to the left side of the wheelchair, and they continued through the store. I bought something so that Leader could practice carrying a shopping bag through the mall, which was one of his favorite things to do.

Even though he was young and had many physical challenges, Martin quickly became an excellent handler. He had an extremely strong connection with Leader and once shared with me that he suspected Leader might actually be a person in a dog's body. Martin was an exceptional student and completed high school at just sixteen years old. He went on to study history at the University of Hawai'i. His faithful friend and copilot, Leader, always remained right by his side.

6

Freedom Saves the Day

Courage is not the absence of fear, but the triumph over it.

Nelson Mandela

A friend who raised show dogs called one day to tell me about a beautiful golden retriever puppy she had seen on Oahu. His parents were both champions, and he had been destined for the show ring before it was discovered that he had a crooked tail.

"They're willing to let him go and love the idea of him being in your program," she said. "He's three months old and is extremely calm and people oriented. There's just something special about him, and I think he might be a good fit for your program."

I flew to Oahu to meet the puppy and, of course, instantly fell in love with him. His coat was a medium gold and he had dark, soulful eyes. The long hair around his neck and chest made him look like he was part lion. He was large for his age and surprisingly calm. He approached me with his tail low and wagging slowly, and sat down right next to me. He gently leaned against my leg and touched my hand with his nose.

"This one always likes to be touching," the breeder said with a laugh. He wasn't needy, though. He had a solid presence that felt comforting, and I thought about how nice this would be for his eventual partner.

He was the first puppy we purchased for our program, and despite his crooked tail, he nearly broke the bank. He came back to Maui with me that night and settled right into our home. We were going through the alphabet naming the puppies and were at the letter *F*. Feanna called that night, and I told her about the new pup. "Why don't you name him Freedom," she suggested, "because that's what he's going to give someone." So, Freedom it was!

The next morning, Will woke me up early with a look on his face that I'd never seen before. "Mo, you need to wake up," he said. "Something terrible has happened."

I sat bolt upright in bed. "Are the dogs okay?"

"Yes, but come and see the TV."

Confused, I followed him into the living room and stopped in my tracks when I saw the unforgettable image of a plane crashing into a tall building.

"America is under attack," Will said.

I watched in utter horror. Tears streamed down my face as the events of the day unfolded. In the days following 9/11, everything seemed so uncertain. I had an unsettling feeling that the world as I knew it would never be the same. Along with fears for our national security, the news was full of dire predictions for the economy. It seemed like a perilous time for any business but especially for a fledgling nonprofit.

The next day, the mall manager let us know they had another tenant for the space we were in and needed us to move. They offered another retail space for us to use, but it was clear we needed something more permanent. As I unpacked the final box in our new office, I dreamed of the day we would have our own campus with exercise fields, walking trails, and dedicated spaces for training the dogs. I decided to contact some of the large landowners on the island to see if anyone would consider donating land to us. In the meantime, I made the best of what we had and worked hard to expand the program.

Freedom's classmate and best friend was Echo, a Portuguese water dog. The two dogs could not have been more different. Echo had lots of energy and loved working. If they were cars, Echo would be a high-performance Maserati, and Freedom would be a comfortable and steady minivan. Will and I prayed that each of them would find his purpose in life.

I went to work each day with Freedom and Echo and took turns teaching them to walk next to the wheelchair around the mall. We often went to the movie theater, where the biggest challenge was teaching them to ignore popcorn on the floor. When Freedom walked next to me, he had an endearing habit of touching my arm with his nose as if to remind me, "I'm right here."

One day, I was sitting at my desk while Echo and Freedom were napping at my feet, and the phone rang. The caller introduced herself as Melanie and said she was interested in applying for a service dog. She explained that she had lost some of her mobility and peripheral vision due to lupus, a disease that causes the immune system to attack the body's organs. Melanie was from Oahu and lived in an apartment near Diamond Head with her husband, Mark, and their two sons. She and her husband met when they both were serving in the army. She'd received a medical discharge, and he was still on active duty. I made an appointment to meet with her the next time I was on Oahu.

I brought Echo with me, thinking his advanced skills might be a good fit for her. Echo and I rode the elevator up to the twenty-fifth floor and knocked on their door. Melanie answered and invited me into their small apartment. She was a lovely Hawaiian woman, with a full figure and glossy black hair that hung in waves around her shoulders. I was more impressed by her inner beauty, which shone through her eyes. Her husband, Mark, was a transplant from Alabama. He wore camouflage army fatigues and had the standard military crew cut. His appearance was a little intimidating at first, but I quickly learned that he was a big softy, especially when it came to Melanie.

Her goals were pretty simple: she was hoping a service dog could help her regain her confidence and independence. She sounded sad as she explained that she hadn't left the house by herself in over ten years. She wanted to be able to go shopping or to the movies while Mark was at work and their boys were at school. She also wanted a dog for companionship because she was often lonely during the day.

After meeting Melanie, I realized Echo would not be the right match for her. I had become experienced at assessing social styles and was pretty sure that Melanie was an "amiable" while Echo was definitely more of a "driver." This wouldn't be a good fit because he was more assertive than she was and not nearly as social. Melanie's personality reminded me a lot of Freedom, who was also an "amiable." They were both easygoing and had a good sense of humor.

We had a growing list of applications for hospital dogs, and I initially thought Freedom might be well suited for this type of work. I wanted to stay open to God's plan for him, so I decided to see if Freedom could learn some of the service dog skills that Melanie needed. He quickly learned to open doors, turn on lights, and retrieve a wallet from a purse.

One evening, Will and I went out to dinner at our favorite beachside restaurant. We brought Freedom with us as part of his training in public places. Patio lights twinkled overhead while Freedom slept under the table. Will and I were deep in thought as we sketched the latest design for our dream campus on a paper napkin. We loved to brainstorm ideas and were always coming up with new plans for its design. Will's technical expertise as an engineer and builder were a big help and the designs kept getting better.

Will was just informing me how much the latest revisions would cost when I felt something solid land on my lap. Looking down, I was astonished to see an expensive-looking red leather wallet. Freedom was looking up at me with a very pleased expression. I stared in disbelief as I picked it up.

"Freedom, where did you get this?" I asked him.

He looked over at the table across from us, where a well-dressed older couple were seated. There was an open purse on the ground next to the woman. Feeling a little like a kleptomaniac, I walked over and asked if the wallet was hers. She said yes and grabbed it quickly from my hand, as I apologized and tried to explain what had happened. Her look implied that she didn't believe me. When I returned to our table, Will joked that we might have discovered a new way of fundraising for the campus.

Freedom was completing the final stages of training for Melanie, but we still didn't have quite the right match for Echo. I was concerned because he wasn't an easy dog to match, so I prayed that we would find the right partner. Days later, we received an application from a young woman named Ann, who was paralyzed from a car accident. She had recently graduated from college and was a competitive wheelchair athlete. When I met with her, I immediately recognized the same drive and determination I saw in Echo. We finished the final stage of training for both dogs and scheduled the team training camp with their new partners.

Melanie and Service/Guide Dog Freedom

When I saw the two teams together for the first time, I tried not to laugh as I recognized how much the two women were the human versions of their canine partners. Team training camp was my favorite part of the entire process. Seeing the dogs bond with their partners and begin their new lives together was always incredibly rewarding. It was nicknamed "boot camp" because the schedule and curriculum were so rigorous. The dogs already knew what they needed to know, but the students had to memorize ninety cues as well as learn all about dog psychology, health care, grooming, and public etiquette.

A friendly rivalry soon developed between Melanie and Ann. Each morning they took written exams, and this was when the competition really escalated. The first day, Melanie looked pleased with her score of 98 percent, until she discovered Ann had scored 99 percent. From then on, each scored over 100 percent, as they aced their exams and received bonus points for extra credit. They graduated from team training camp and began their new lives with their canine companions.

The two women had opposite personalities but became fast friends. We were invited to attend Mark and Melanie's vow renewal the following year. Ann was the maid of honor, Freedom was the best man, and Echo was their ring bearer.

With Freedom's help, Melanie slowly regained her confidence and independence. She began volunteering at her sons' school and enjoyed going shopping and to the movies. She called from the mall one day to ask if she could buy a Coach collar for Freedom because they found one that "he" really liked. Apparently, Freedom had progressed from a pickpocket to a dog with expensive taste. They attended matinees together and once, during a particularly frightening scene in a movie,

Freedom jumped onto Melanie's lap. After that, she was convinced he was afraid of scary movies, and they only watched comedies together from then on.

When he was three years old, Freedom attended a formal military ball with Melanie and Mark. It was held at an ocean-front resort in Waikiki, and the ballroom was filled with fresh flowers and candlelight. Melanie wore a beautiful red evening gown, and Mark wore a tuxedo. Freedom looked very dapper in his black bow tie and, of course, was a perfect gentleman throughout the evening. The three of them had their photo taken, and when Melanie sent it to me, it brought tears to my eyes. Seeing Melanie navigate the world with Freedom on her left side and Mark on her right was a beautiful sight. She now had two men in her life who were completely devoted to her.

About a year later, I was walking on Haleakala Ranch, looking at a possible location for our campus. My phone buzzed, and I saw there was a message from Mark.

"This is Mark," he said, his voice shaking on the recording. "Please call me right away."

My heart lurched. I called him back and tried to stay calm. Melanie had many health complications from lupus, and I felt a sense of foreboding. Mark was choked up as he answered the phone, and I feared the worst. When he could finally speak, he explained there had been a house fire that day when Melanie was home alone. He also thanked me, though I didn't know why, and said that Melanie wanted to talk to me.

"Hi, Mo," she whispered.

"Are you okay?" I asked.

"Yes," she replied. "I was cooking this afternoon and the stove caught on fire."

I gasped.

"I tried to stop it," she said. "But the flames kept getting bigger."

"Oh, Melanie!" I exclaimed.

"My hair caught on fire," she said, her voice shaking. "And when I tried to put out the flames, my wheelchair tipped over. I was trapped underneath."

My heart pounded as Melanie described the scene. I sat down on a fallen log as she described what happened next. She lay facedown on the cold tile floor, unable to move, as the flames grew and the room filled with smoke. She thought it was the end, but then she felt a cold nose nudging her. She looked into Freedom's eyes, which were full of concern. Trying to stay calm, she said, "Freedom, go find the phone."

Melanie didn't know where to tell him to look, and he returned a few minutes later, carrying a stuffed animal and sheepishly wagging his tail in apology. She took the toy from his mouth and looked intently into his eyes. "Phone," she said. "Go find the phone!"

He ran off again in search of it. She heard him running up and down the stairs and looking all over the house. Minutes later, he appeared through the smoke carrying the phone in his mouth.

"Good boy, Freedom," she cried as he placed it in her hand and she called 911. When the firefighters arrived, the flames were closing in and Melanie was gasping for breath. She barely managed to tell Freedom, "Go, tug." He ran to the living room and tugged the rope on the front door handle and pulled open the door. He led the firefighters directly to Melanie.

"I just got home from the hospital and you're the first person I called. They let Freedom ride in the ambulance with me.

I have some first-degree burns and smoke inhalation, but I'll be fine," she said.

I stared out across the pasture and imagined what Freedom was thinking and feeling as he frantically searched for the phone. The sight of Melanie lying on the floor and the smell of burned hair and smoke must have terrified him. I was thankful he was able to stay focused and complete his task in the face of such extreme distractions. I shuddered to think what might have happened if he hadn't succeeded.

"Are you still there, Mo?" Melanie asked.

"Yes, I'm here. I'm just so glad you're okay."

"Do you know what the most surprising thing was?"

"What?"

"It wasn't that Freedom brought me the phone or opened the door; I already knew he could do that. What amazed me was that after I called 911, he lay right down next to me. Even though the fire was getting closer and the smoke was getting worse, I could tell he wasn't going to leave me," she said through her tears. "Freedom is my hero. I wouldn't be alive if it weren't for him."

By the time Melanie finished, I was weeping right along with her. I thanked God that Freedom had found his purpose and was there when she needed him most.

Their bond grew even stronger over time. A few years later, Mark was transferred to a military base on the mainland that was near his family in Alabama. Not long after, Melanie called to tell me that she had completely lost her sight due to complications from lupus. She was attending a school for the blind and was learning how to read braille and function without her sight. I encouraged her to apply for a guide dog, but she wouldn't hear of it. She insisted that she didn't want any other dog but Freedom. He continued to help her out at home, but she had once again lost her independence.

During their next annual follow-up report, I asked her one of the standard questions: "Where does Freedom sleep at night?" My pen was poised to fill in the usual answer that he slept on his dog bed, right next to hers.

"He sleeps on top of me," she replied.

"Um, you mean he sleeps next to you on your bed?" I clarified.

"No," she said. "When I lost my sight, I became disoriented at night and started falling out of bed. Freedom got upset when this happened, so he started sleeping right on top of me. He thought of it all on his own, and I haven't fallen out of bed since."

Eventually, the loss of Melanie's eyesight prompted them to move back to Hawaii, where family and friends could help her adjust. I went to visit them at their house on the military base. It broke my heart to discover she was more afraid to go outside than she had been the first time we met years before. Melanie desperately wanted her independence back, so we came up with a plan—she'd travel with her white cane on the right side, while Freedom walked on her left. She already knew how to use the cane to avoid obstacles and asked if I would teach Freedom to help her find specific locations. This was not exactly my area of expertise, but how could I say no?

Rule #6: ~~Train service dogs to assist those with limited mobility.~~

Once again, her dream was to go to the grocery store by herself so she could shop for her family. I drove the mile to the grocery store with her and described the route in detail so she could visualize it. There were two small side streets they would have to cross in the beginning before they got to the biggest hurdle: a busy intersection with six lanes of traffic. Once they got past this, it was a straight shot to the store with only a few small streets to cross.

During our first training session, we had just reached the sidewalk in front of her house when the first car whizzed by. Melanie began to shake uncontrollably and broke out in a sweat.

"I'm sorry, Mo; I can't do this," she said. "They sound so close." We turned around and continued on a paved path through her complex, and she slowly began to relax.

I returned the next week and chose midday when there wouldn't be as much traffic. We started out on the tree-lined path through her complex. Freedom heeled on Melanie's left side, and she held her white cane on the right and swept it back and forth in front of her. She agreed to try the sidewalk again, and we slowly went down her driveway. I walked behind her with my hand resting on her shoulder.

"You're doing great. You've got this!" I closed my eyes and listened as the first car drove past us. I imagined myself in her place, sitting in the wheelchair, unable to move or see. I noticed the cars sounded much louder when I couldn't see them. Freedom remained calm and focused.

We made it half a block to the first intersection when a truck sped by us. I recognized the look on Melanie's face and saw the sweat start to trickle down her cheeks.

"I need to go home," she whispered, and we quickly turned back. For the next couple of months, progress was slow but steady as we continued practicing and getting closer to the busy intersection.

One weekend, when Will and I were both there, Melanie announced that she was ready to try crossing the busy intersection that was on the way to the store. We stood on either side of her at the curb and waved cars on as she sat and listened carefully to the traffic patterns. There were a total of six lanes, and it was difficult for her to get a sense of traffic flow. We crossed with her a few times and were amazed by her determination and the courage she summoned to overcome her fear.

The next day she wanted to go back to the same intersection and try it again. We stood with her at the curb as cars whizzed by. When the light turned green, we began to walk with her across the street, but she put out her hand to stop us. "Please wait here. I want to do this alone."

Will and I stood on the curb and watched like nervous parents as she and Freedom set out on their own to cross the street, which suddenly looked a mile wide. Finally, they made it to the other side, and we both breathed a huge sigh of relief while we waited for the light to change so we could catch up with them. We were so proud of Melanie, and both of us had tears in our eyes when we reached her.

Will gave her a big hug, and I said, "Melanie, that was the most wonderful thing I've ever seen!" Will wholeheartedly agreed.

She raised her eyebrows and shook her head. "You two really need to get out more."

We all burst out laughing and Freedom looked delighted.

Melanie's independence grew over the years, and she ventured to many more places with Freedom by her side. She called to share their triumphs each time they went somewhere new. I saw their bond grow stronger with each passing year.

When Freedom was ten years old, Mark was deployed back to Iraq. He said he was confident going because he knew that Melanie would be safe at home with Freedom. When Mark returned from the war, Will and I visited them on Oahu. They couldn't believe how excited Freedom was when he saw us. No matter how old the dogs get, there is always a part of them that remembers their puppy days and the love we shared. Mark and Melanie sat close together on their couch holding hands while we visited.

"You two look just as in love as ever!" I said with a smile.

"Sorry Mo, but you'll have to speak up a bit," said Mark. "I lost some of my hearing when I was in Iraq this time. We're quite the pair, aren't we?" he laughed.

"That's right," Melanie quipped. "We've discovered the secret to a happy marriage. I can't see him, and he can't hear me!" Freedom heard us all laughing and slowly got up and walked over to Melanie. He nudged her hand with his white muzzle as if to say, *I'm right here*. She rested her hand on his head and smiled down at him. Although she couldn't see him, his cloudy eyes gazed steadily back at her. The look of pure love they shared went much deeper than sight.

7

Oliver, aka Mr. Mom

*Whoever said that diamonds were a girl's best friend . . .
never had a dog.*

Anonymous

Two sets of friendly dark eyes looked at me through the thin
metal grate of the kennel door. I was once again at the Kahului Airport, welcoming our newest arrivals. The travelers
who hustled and bustled around me were too busy hurrying
to their next adventure to notice me as I crouched in front of
the kennel in the corner of the baggage claim area.

I caught a whiff of puppy breath and my heart melted. I
reached my fingers through the cold grate and felt the sleek,
silky ears of the black puppy. She looked cautious but didn't
back away. The big yellow boy bumped up next to her, grinning from ear to ear and wagging his tail in excitement. They

were born just a week apart and would be classmates for the next year and a half.

We named the boy Oliver and the girl Penny. She was also known as Miss Money Penny, which seemed appropriate since they came all the way from England and cost a small fortune. After losing our own dog Bart to cancer at just five years old, I was determined to prevent that kind of heartache for our clients. I researched the best lines of Labradors, which took us all the way to England. We visited the top show breeders who also selected for temperament and carefully screened their dogs for health issues like cancer, blindness, and hip dysplasia.

Oliver's and Penny's personalities were as different as their appearances. He was confident and outgoing while she was quiet and demure. A few days after they arrived, we performed temperament evaluations on both puppies. There were fifteen exercises that helped us gauge things like assertiveness, retrieve instinct, confidence, and sound sensitivity. We started with Penny, who sat where she was placed in the middle of the room and didn't move. She looked around and contemplated the unfamiliar surroundings. Then she stood up and walked toward me with her tail held low and slowly wagging. She sat next to me and leaned against my leg. When I crumpled up a piece of paper and flicked it across the floor, she took a step or two toward it and then changed her mind and returned to my side. When Will dropped a notebook on the floor ten feet away, Penny startled momentarily but quickly recovered.

When it was Oliver's turn, Will set him down in the same spot in the middle of the room. He sprang up immediately and began investigating everything in the room with his tail held high and wagging quickly. He discovered a floor mat, which he dragged a few feet, and then he ran around the room. Oliver watched closely as I scrunched up the paper, and he sprang after it when I flicked it across the floor. He pounced on it and carried it right back to me. When Will dropped the notebook, he spun around and investigated it with a wide tail-wag.

Perhaps the most telling exercise is how the puppies react when placed on their backs. This is a submissive posture, and the puppies who are more assertive tend not to tolerate it as well. I sat on the floor with my legs straight out in front of me. I placed Penny on my lap and gently rolled her over onto her back. She immediately relaxed and her legs went completely limp as I rubbed her tummy. When it was Oliver's turn, he allowed me to roll him over but wiggled a little before he re-laxed. As I petted his chest, he smiled and looked directly at me, which showed his confidence.

Despite their different temperaments, both puppies scored well on the tests. As with people, each dog has its own per-sonality and strengths. My job is to understand each one and help them reach their full potential. It would be another year before they were matched with a partner, but I suspected that Penny's sensitivity might make her well suited as a home com-panion for a child with special needs, while Oliver's drive and enthusiasm would make him a good candidate for someone who was active and needed a service dog with strong skills.

Shortly after Oliver and Penny went to their puppy-raising homes, I received a phone call from the bank with the most wonderful news. A generous benefactor had donated the funds for us to purchase the land we had been looking at on Haleakala Ranch. Will and I couldn't believe it—our dream of building an Assistance Dogs campus was about to become a reality! We began spending every weekend at the property with the puppies-in-training, walking through the eucalyptus forest and deciding where to construct the buildings we had been dreaming about for years.

I continued to work at our office at the mall during this time and often welcomed guests who stopped by to visit the puppies. Two regular visitors were Monica and her four-year-old daughter, Ava. They found out about our program when Ava was a patient at the children's hospital and we visited with Tucker. Ava was a beautiful little girl with sandy blonde hair and hazel eyes framed perfectly by long, dark eyelashes. She was born with spina bifida, a birth defect that causes the spinal cord not to form properly. She also had considerable sensitivities to movement and sound.

Monica inquired about a service dog for Ava, and I let her know the minimum age requirement was ten years old. However, I offered for them to visit anytime so Ava could get more comfortable around dogs. When they first came to the office, Ava was so afraid she hid in one of the dog crates and closed the gate. She covered her ears with her hands and squeezed her eyes closed while she rocked back and forth. Oliver was fascinated by Ava and watched her closely each time they visited. Monica continued to bring Ava by the office, and she slowly became more relaxed around the dogs.

Oliver was such a happy pup and was always the life of the party during puppy classes and field trips. His enthusiasm and cheerfulness were hard to resist. At home, he provided Will and me with endless entertainment. Once, we were watching a movie and he came racing through the living room with a roll of toilet paper streaming behind him. Another time, we were hosting a dinner party when all of a sudden everyone started laughing. I looked around and was horrified to see that Oliver was proudly parading around the table with my bra in his mouth. Oliver was a comedian at heart, and there was no greater reward for him than to make people laugh!

At twelve months old, Oliver's life as he knew it was about to change. We had just bred our first litter of puppies and were blessed with the arrival of eleven healthy golden retrievers. Will had built a custom wooden whelping box, where the puppies were born and spent the first few weeks of their lives. We placed it in front of the big stone fireplace in the living room of our upcountry home. Unfortunately, the puppies' mother was not as thrilled by their arrival as we were. She only went into the whelping box to nurse them, and even then it took some coaxing from us. Although they had an absentee mom, Oliver could not have been more attentive. He watched the puppies nonstop for the first few days. He wouldn't let them out of his sight, so we moved his dog bed right next to the whelping box. At night, he slept with his chin resting on the edge of it.

During the day, he hung his head over the edge of the box and studied the puppies' every move. Their eyes and ears wouldn't open for another two weeks, but they could smell milk and feel the warmth of their mother's body. One day, the puppies were crying and searching for their mom. It was too much for Oliver, and he decided it was time to make his move. He tiptoed into the box, like he'd watched their mother do, and carefully lay down. The puppies sensed his presence and climbed all over him, looking for milk. He couldn't help in that department, but he licked them all over and even helped clean up their messes. From then on, Oliver spent most of his time in the box with the puppies and became affectionately known as "Mr. Mom."

The puppies couldn't leave our house or yard until they received their vaccinations, so Oliver was in quarantine right along with them. Each puppy wore a different color collar to help us tell them apart. The agreement with the dam's owner was that we would keep three puppies to train as assistance dogs. They would sell the others as pets, but we were responsible for finding and screening the families. This seemed reasonable at the time, but when the puppies were eight weeks old and it came time for them to leave, it somehow felt like we were selling our own children. We selected Sarge, Sadie, and Simba for the program, and the other puppies went to their new homes. All except for Sam, that is. He was the big pup with the red collar who had captured our hearts. We were reluctant to give him up and took a little extra time interviewing families for him.

Oliver finished his "pawternity" leave and returned to school. Penny and his other classmates were thrilled to have him back, as things had been pretty quiet without him. Oliver excelled in the class and quickly learned to tug open doors, carry a lunch box, and retrieve a variety of items. He had grown into a big, strong dog, and I wondered who his eventual partner would be.

During this time, Will was busy overseeing the permit process and site preparation for the new campus. I started applying for grants to help pay for the campus construction. It seemed like a daunting task to raise so much money, but I squashed my fears and trusted that God would provide as we stepped out in faith. It was so encouraging when the first few grants began trickling in from local foundations and the support for our campus grew. We were determined not to go into debt, so we moved forward with the project at the same rate at which we received donations.

Eventually, Oliver was matched with an applicant named Dave. He was an outgoing young man with an expressive personality like Oliver's. He had a spinal cord injury and used a manual wheelchair, so I began teaching Oliver how to pull a wheelchair. He wore a special leather pulling harness that had a handle on each side. While Oliver was heeling next to the chair, I'd hold the handle on his harness and say, "Oliver, pull." He'd lean his barrel chest into the harness and eagerly forge ahead. It was an incredible feeling of freedom not to have to push the wheelchair, and Oliver loved doing it!

Team training camp was a month away when Dave had a family emergency and had to return to the mainland. They had seemed like such a great match and I was disappointed by the news. This was the first of many times I discovered that when my plans for a dog didn't work out, it was because God had something even better in mind. It turned out, the answer had been right in front of us all along.

The following day, Monica and Ava stopped by the office on their way home from a doctor's appointment. Monica looked exhausted and shared that Ava's seizures had become more frequent. She was worried that Ava might fall and be injured during a seizure, so she never let Ava out of her sight.

As we talked, I watched Ava use her arms to scoot across the office floor.

"Oliver, follow me," she said with a smile. The plastic braces on her legs made a scratching sound as they slid across the ceramic-tile floor. She crawled onto Oliver's dog bed and lay down. He followed closely behind and curled up next to her, just as he had done with the puppies. He carefully rested his head across her tiny torso, and she wrapped her little arms around his neck. He had a look of pure contentment that I hadn't seen since he was in the whelping box with the puppies. Could this be his match? Ava couldn't have been more different than Dave, and there was that rule about the ten-year age minimum. But I had learned not to let my own rules or expectations get in the way of what God was doing.

"When Ava is old enough to get a service dog, what are the things you'd like a dog to help her with?" I asked Monica, trying my best to sound nonchalant.

"Oh, there are so many," she replied. "It would be great if a dog could help her walk and maybe help get her medicine and turn on lights that she can't reach. It would also just be nice for her to have a companion, since she doesn't have any siblings."

"What about letting you know if a seizure is starting?"

Her eyes widened. "Do you really think a dog could do that?" she asked.

"Yes, dogs can learn to recognize when a seizure is starting and bark to alert someone."

"That would be amazing," she replied. "That means I could be in the kitchen cooking dinner while Ava plays in her room. It would help us both to be more independent."

She described what Ava's seizures were like and showed me how they started, with the flicking of her finger. The seizures progressed to Ava's arm, and eventually her entire body would be affected by a grand mal seizure.

As soon as they left the office, I invited Oliver to join me where I was sitting at my desk. I looked intently into his shiny dark eyes and began flicking my pointer finger just as Monica had demonstrated. He cocked his head and gave me a quizzical look, as if to say, *I'm not sure what that means.* I repeated the movement and said, "Speak." This was a cue he already knew, so he barked in reply. Next, I combined the physical and verbal cues and rewarded him with a treat for the correct response. Finally, I did just the finger flick and he barked on cue. I couldn't wait to show Monica.

The next time they visited the office, I sat with Monica while we watched Ava play with Oliver. "What would you think about Oliver being Ava's dog?" I asked.

"I think it would be a miracle," she replied.

"What do you mean?"

"Well, lately, when Ava says her prayers at night, she has been asking if Oliver could be her dog." And with that, another rule went by the wayside.

Rule #7: Minimum age requirement is ten years old.

During the first week of team training camp, we practiced in the office and around the mall. Oliver was the biggest dog we'd ever had at eighty-two pounds, and Ava was the smallest client at just twenty-eight pounds. Oliver was thrilled to finally have a child of his own and was completely enamored with Ava. At the end of the week, it was time for him to go home with his new family. I hugged them goodbye and watched from the doorway as they headed toward the parking lot. Monica pushed Ava's wheelchair, and Oliver walked proudly beside them. I struggled to control my emotions as I watched them leave. Oliver suddenly stopped and turned around. He looked back at me with a joyous smile, and I knew he had found his purpose. I waved goodbye to him and they disappeared around the corner.

The second week of team training took place at their home in the small surf town of Paia on the north shore of Maui. They lived in a plantation house that was originally built for the workers who tended the sugarcane fields. I laughed when

I saw where Oliver slept. He was such a masculine dog, and everything in Ava's room was pink and fairy princess themed. She had a child-sized bed that she was convinced was big enough to share with Oliver, or Ollie, as she liked to call him. Monica knew when Ava woke up each morning, because she heard her giggling and the thump, thump, thump of Ollie's tail against the wall. Monica also shared that Ava's seizures had become much less frequent since Ollie's arrival.

Together, we practiced various tasks that Ollie would assist Ava with throughout the day. At the end of the week, they took their final working exam. I stood in the corner and watched as they demonstrated their morning routine.

"Ollie, light," Ava said from her bed, and he walked across the room and touched the light switch on the wall with his nose to turn it on.

"Get my braces," she said, and he went to the closet and picked up both of her tiny leg braces in his mouth and placed them on her bed. "Thank you, Ollie," she said and gave him a kiss on top of his head. Monica slipped on her leg braces and tightened the Velcro straps.

"Ollie, get my clothes," Ava said, and he walked over to her little pink dresser and tugged on the rope I had tied to the knob of the top drawer. He carefully took out the clothes Monica had selected the night before. "Good boy, Ollie!" Ava said as he carried them to her and placed them on the bed.

"Push," she said, and he went back and closed the drawer with his paw. She had a huge smile, and I could tell how proud she was of Ollie.

Finally, she said, "Get my shoes," and he walked to her closet and picked up her tennis shoes in his mouth. One fell to the floor and when he reached down to get it, he accidentally picked up the wrong shoe. He carried the mismatched shoes and proudly deposited them on her lap.

"Good boy, Ollie," she said softly.

"I'll bring you the other one," I offered.

"No, that's okay; I'll just wear these," she said. "Ollie tried so hard, and I don't want to hurt his feelings."

During her physical therapy sessions, Ollie wore a leather harness with a short, rigid handle above his shoulders. He learned how to "step" and "wait" so he could help Ava practice walking. She held on to his harness and together they slowly took one step at a time.

Ava became upset each time she had to take medications during the day. I asked if she would like Ollie to bring her medicine, and her face lit up. We placed her medicine in a

Service / Seizure Response Dog Oliver and Ava

paper lunch bag, and Ollie retrieved it from the bathroom counter. Taking her medicine suddenly became a game that she looked forward to!

Each night when Ava went to bed, Ollie brought her a book from her desk across the room and Monica read them a bedtime story. The three of them snuggled together on the pink quilt, and Ava fell asleep hugging Ollie. Monica gave them each a kiss good night and whispered, "Thank you, Ollie," before turning out the light.

The first time Monica heard Oliver bark, she was folding laundry in the living room. She was surprised at first and then remembered. She dropped the shirt she was folding and ran into Ava's room. She found Ava lying on the floor and Oliver standing over her looking anxious. Monica spoke soothingly even though she knew Ava couldn't hear her. A few minutes later, when the seizure stopped and she came to, Ollie looked relieved and kissed Ava's cheek.

During her first year with Ollie, Ava's sensory issues improved tremendously. Monica believed that having such a big, affectionate dog next to her all the time had helped desensitize Ava to other stimuli in the environment. This was a huge and unexpected benefit of having Oliver.

Part of the annual follow-up visits for each team includes making sure the dogs are healthy and well groomed. The clients have daily, weekly, and monthly routines for their dogs, which include brushing their coat, brushing their teeth, cleaning their ears, and trimming their nails. I noticed during one of their annual follow-up visits that Oliver's teeth were exceptionally white, especially for an older dog. I asked Monica how often she brushed them.

"Twice a day," she replied. "I started using an electric tooth-brush a while back, since that seems to get them cleaner. Oh, and I hope it's okay, I also floss his teeth every day."

I went home from the visit impressed with her conscien-tious care of Oliver—and with a vague feeling that I could probably step up my own grooming routine.

As Ava grew up, Ollie provided her with confidence and was a bridge to help her connect with other people. She was so proud of him and loved watching people's reactions when she demonstrated his skills.

Every year on Ollie's birthday, Monica and Ava made him a special birthday cake out of dog food and avocado, with shaved carrots on top. They all wore birthday hats and Ollie waited patiently while they sang "Happy Birthday" to him before diving into his birthday cake.

Ava became a dynamo as she got older and enjoyed partici-pating in several sports. She learned how to play wheelchair tennis and even competed in surfing competitions. She was a bit of a daredevil and loved having Oliver pull her fast in her wheelchair, which made me nervous. I didn't need to worry, though, because Oliver always made sure his little girl was safe and remained devoted to her throughout his life.

When he was fifteen years old, Oliver's mission on earth was complete. Monica called to let me know that he went home peacefully on Christmas Day. The following week, they came up to the campus to spread his ashes on the Freedom Trail. It broke my heart to see Ava sitting in her wheelchair, sobbing as she held his urn on her lap. Although I knew what a blessing Oliver had been, I wished she could have avoided this heartache. But even through her sorrow, I could see a newfound confidence and strength in Ava. A strength that I knew Oliver had helped her to achieve.

"Ava, I will spread his ashes for you if it makes you too sad," I offered.

"Thank you, but I want to do it," she said. "Ollie was always there for me, and I want to be there for him this one last time."

8

Miss Money Penny

Life is 10% what happens to you and 90% how you react to it.

Charles R. Swindoll

Construction of the new campus was in full swing. Saws buzzed and the smell of freshly cut lumber filled the air as we stood inside the framing of the building we had dreamed about for years. Will was in his element helping with the construction and overseeing the subcontractors. I was beyond excited for the campus to be completed, as we had a growing list of applicants and were bursting at the seams with more puppies-in-training than ever before. We'd recently hired our first employee and she was a gem. Donna worked as our office manager, helping to answer the phones, pay bills, and greet guests. She also helped to oversee our growing community outreach program, where we took the puppies-in-training to visit local hospitals, nursing homes, and homeless shelters. I was busy writing grant proposals for the campus one day when Donna put a call on hold and asked, "Do you have time to take a call from a potential client?"

"Sure," I replied, closing my laptop. I enjoyed talking with applicants and was thrilled when it was someone we might be able to help. The hardest part was not being able to assist everyone who called.

"Hi, this is Mo. How may I help you?"

"Aloha," said a friendly voice. "My name is Angie and I'm calling from Lanai. I'd like to apply for a service dog for my eight-year-old son, Mikey."

Angie described her son's condition, which resulted from a near-drowning accident when he was twenty months old. My heart broke for her as she explained how the lack of oxygen resulted in complete paralysis, along with severe vision and hearing impairment. She shared that Mikey also had frequent seizures. She was hoping that a service dog might enhance Mikey's quality of life and provide companionship for him. I was so impressed by Angie's positive attitude despite the challenges she faced. I wasn't exactly sure how a dog would assist Mikey, but by the end of the call, I knew that I wanted to help.

We received Mikey's application the following week. Since he was completely paralyzed, there weren't as many physical tasks a dog could help him with, like picking up objects or bringing the phone. I decided to focus on the seizure response skill since that had been such a big help for Ava. We tested our dogs-in-training to see if any had an aptitude for this type of work.

Donna brought the dogs into the training room one at a time. After she left, I simulated a seizure by falling to the floor and moving my arms and legs. The first dog was a big black lab named Marshal. He stared at me for a moment and then walked to the door, clearly wanting out! The next dog was a friendly yellow lab named Hoku. She got very excited when she saw me on the floor. She jumped on me and started frantically pawing. Since the purpose was to prevent injuries during a seizure and not to inflict them, we halted this trial right away.

The next candidate was a six-month-old golden retriever named Vinny. He looked concerned as I fell to the floor, and he hovered over me for a moment. *That's more like it*, I thought. *He's analyzing the situation before deciding how to proceed.* Then he tiptoed away, covertly glancing back at me lying on the floor. He jumped up on the treat table and tried to steal some dog biscuits. "Next!" I called, and Donna took Vinny out and brought in the final contestant.

Penny ambled into the room in her typical demure and unassuming fashion. I waited until she wasn't watching and then fell to the floor. She rushed over to me and touched my hand with her wet nose. Then she sat down next to me and looked around the room for help. I kept moving my arms and legs and waited to see what would happen next. She circled my body twice, softly whining and nudging me. Finally, she lay down beside me and nuzzled my face and gently licked my cheek. I opened my eyes and stopped moving my arms and legs. I saw a look of profound relief on her face, and I quietly praised her. Penny demonstrated both a concern for people and good body awareness, which are essential for seizure response.

Penny was fifteen months old and in the advanced training class with her best friend, Oliver. She loved children and was very intuitive, so I thought she might be a good fit for Mikey.

She was smaller than most of our dogs and had a sleek coat and soft, rabbit-like ears.

I scheduled the home interview with Angie and picked up Penny from her devoted puppy raiser, Kimmy. We drove to the town of Lahaina on the west side of Maui and boarded a small passenger ferry for the one-hour trip to the island of Lanai. Penny and I sat up top where there were a few seats for those of us who wanted to enjoy the fresh air and sea spray. The sun warmed my face as we departed Lahaina Harbor. The rugged West Maui Mountains loomed over the town as we slowly pulled out of the harbor. Back in the 1800s, Lahaina was the capital of Hawaii and a major seaport. Many original buildings still remain, especially along the waterfront.

As Maui faded into the distance and Lanai drew closer, my excitement to explore this mysterious island grew. The mountaintop was surrounded by clouds, and no signs of civilization could be seen from the boat. We reached the middle of the Auau Channel, and the waves started to pick up. I suddenly realized the other passengers had all moved below and Penny and I were alone. The boat lurched violently up the crest of an oncoming wave and crashed down into the trough. Hanging on to the railing with white knuckles, I began to look at Lanai differently. I wondered, *If the boat were to capsize, would Penny and I be able to swim to shore?* We were about a half mile offshore, so I thought we'd have a pretty decent chance. I imagined Penny and me swimming side by side to the deserted coastline and pulling ourselves up onto the rocky shore. I pictured Will when he got the tragic news that the boat had sunk and there were no survivors. However, he would refuse to give up hope and would come looking for us. Suddenly a wave crashed over the bow of the boat and completely drenched us, bringing me abruptly back to the present and my actual predicament.

"Penny, let's go," I said, trying to sound confident as I stood up.

One hand gripped her leash and the other clutched a railing as we inched our way toward the stairs. We slowly descended the steps and made it to the stern of the boat where the diesel fumes from the engine were strongest. I began to feel nauseous. We went inside the main cabin, where there were several rows of benches with an aisle in the middle. I was surprised to see that the local commuters seemed oblivious to our peril as I stumbled onto a bench in the back row. I tried to suppress my mounting queasiness by looking at the horizon, but the crashing waves covered the windows as the boat lurched up and down. After a few minutes, I realized that I hadn't seen the sky for a while and wondered if we were still above water or below.

I looked around at the other passengers to see if anyone was aware that the boat was sinking. To my amazement, one man was reading the newspaper, and another was sleeping! I looked down at Penny to see how she was faring and noticed she didn't look so good. Her ears were back and she was staring straight ahead with squinted eyes. She began making a sucking sound and her cheeks started moving in and out.

"Oh no, Penny, please don't," I whispered just before she leaned forward with a loud retching sound and vomited all over the floor. This got everyone's attention. All eyes were suddenly on us. I avoided their gaze by looking down at the floor, which was a big mistake—because then I threw up also. There are times my job can be quite glamorous, but this was definitely not one of them. I got the doggie cleanup kit out of my backpack and went to work. When the ferry docked, I mustered the remains of my dignity as Penny and I departed the vessel and made our way to the rental car.

We drove up to Lanai City, which is actually a small town with a population of about three thousand people. I made a wrong turn and we ended up taking a scenic drive around Dole Park in the center of town. It was a beautiful park with grassy fields and towering Norfolk pine trees. Several local businesses and small shops lined the streets surrounding it. The rest of the town consisted mainly of plantation houses that had originally been built for the workers in the pineapple fields. I parked in front of Angie's home, which was perched on the hill above town and had a well-manicured front yard.

Angie greeted us at the door with a welcoming smile.

"I'm Mo and this is Penny, one of our dogs-in-training."

"Oh, she's so beautiful," Angie said as she reached down to pet her. Penny smiled at the compliment and wagged her tail in reply.

We followed Angie into their living room where Mikey lay on a futon placed in the middle of the floor. He lay completely motionless and was surrounded by medical equipment. He had a cherubic face with pale skin and light blond hair. His clear blue eyes didn't appear to focus, and I wasn't sure if he was aware of our presence in the room.

"This is Mikey," Angie said brightly as we approached him.

"Hi Mikey. I'm Mo," I said, kneeling down next to him. I wondered how Penny would respond and watched in amazement as she approached him without hesitation. She lay down next to Mikey on the futon and rested her head across his stomach. I looked up at Angie to see if this was okay, and she was smiling through her tears. I reached out and held Mikey's hand in mine. He had the softest skin I had ever felt. While

Angie and I talked, Penny never took her eyes off Mikey's face. It was as if her soul saw his and said, *Oh, there you are! I've been waiting for you.*

Angie showed us the rest of their home and their fenced backyard where Penny could play. On the way back to the living room, Penny discovered a stuffed animal on the floor. She picked it up and took it to Mikey and dropped it on his chest. When she didn't get a reaction, she gently nudged it toward his face with her nose, trying to engage him. I was wondering if this was safe, when suddenly Mikey made a loud honking noise. I looked over at Angie in alarm.

"Is he okay?"

"He's laughing!" she said as her eyes filled with tears. "We hardly ever get to hear that sound."

In addition to being a sympathetic puker, I'm also a sympathetic crier. However, I know the people we serve are looking for assistance, not pity, and I have a strict policy not to cry in front of them. My hope is to bring them joy and to be a light in a dark place. That's hard to do if I let the sadness of the situation overcome me. I kept it together and continued with the interview process.

Angie's husband, Mike, came home from work at lunchtime and was delighted to meet Penny. I asked them if there were specific tasks they wanted a dog to perform for Mikey. They said that more than anything, they wanted a friend for him. They wanted a dog who would sleep with Mikey and go for walks with him as they pushed his stroller-style wheelchair. They also wanted a dog to assist with things like getting Mikey's clothes from the cabinet or bringing a diaper when needed. Angie asked if a dog could help alert them to Mikey's seizures, which happened several times a day. I didn't make any guarantees about this, since his seizures were subtle and I thought Penny might become desensitized to them since they happened so often. I took pictures of everything, including his wheelchair, so I could simulate their environment while completing Penny's training back on Maui.

Before leaving, I sat down by Mikey to say goodbye and held his soft, pale hand in mine. Penny went to the same spot as before and lay next to him. Angie had explained the main way Mikey perceived the world was through his sense of touch. I gently placed Mikey's hand on Penny's ear and moved it back and forth, so he could feel how velvety soft it was. I closed my eyes and said a silent prayer.

"He's looking at her!" Angie exclaimed.

I opened my eyes and saw that Mikey's eyes were deliberately moving to the left in Penny's direction. Mike said that getting Mikey's eyes to track an object was the main goal of his current therapy sessions. I realized then that dogs can help people in so many different ways and that encouraging Mikey to move his eyes was just as important as retrieving an item or opening a door.

Mike and Angie walked me to the car and gave me a big hug as we said goodbye. Penny jumped in the passenger seat and smiled out the window at them as we drove away. I made it about two blocks before I pulled over to the curb and burst into tears. Penny leaned toward me and lifted a dainty paw in consolation. I held her paw in my hand while I said a prayer for Mikey, and that Penny would be able to help him.

Back on Maui, I began teaching Penny specialized skills to assist Mikey. This was my favorite part of training, when I could picture the person whom the dog would be helping. I found a used stroller-style wheelchair, and Penny walked beautifully beside it as we practiced on the sidewalks of the neighborhood near the mall. I endured some suspicious looks from strangers as I pushed the empty stroller past their houses with Penny trotting happily alongside. I smiled and tried my best to look sane.

Penny soon learned to open doors, get a cloth from a cupboard, and carry items. Angie had sent me a video of Mikey having a seizure, and Penny learned to bark when I simulated his movements. Penny also learned to "go find Mom" and alert Angie when Mikey was in distress by nudging her with her nose.

Angie came to Maui to attend the first week of team training camp at our office in the shopping mall. Will had been working tirelessly on the new campus and it was nearing completion. We had recently run out of funds for the project and a substantial amount was still needed to pay for the parking lot, painting, appliances, and furniture. I had written grants to all the local foundations and didn't know where else to turn.

One afternoon, I was in the middle of training with Angie and Penny when a distinguished-looking gentleman paid an unexpected visit to our office. He apologized for the interruption and said he was just there to drop off an envelope. At the end of the day, I sat alone at my desk and opened the envelope. I couldn't believe my eyes—it contained a check for the largest donation we had ever received. Best of all, it was the exact amount we needed to complete the campus. God had miraculously provided once again!

The next week I traveled to Lanai for the second week of training with Mikey and Penny. We practiced mainly at their home but also walked around their neighborhood each day. We even went to the elementary school to give a presentation

Mikey and Service Dog Penny

about disabilities and service dogs. The *Lanai Times* featured a story about Mikey and Penny, and they became instant celebrities in town. I was impressed with how devoted Penny already was to Mikey. She seemed reluctant to ever leave him and, as soon as she finished eating or going outside, immediately rushed back to be by his side.

A few months later, Penny nudged Angie's arm in the middle of the night and woke her up.

"It's not morning yet; go back to sleep," Angie mumbled. Penny persisted and started whining. "What is it, girl, do you need to go outside?" Angie asked as she reluctantly got out of bed. Rather than going to the sliding door, Penny ran down the hallway back to Mikey. Angie followed her and when she got to Mikey, she found he was not breathing and his skin had turned blue. She quickly activated the suction machine next to his bed and cleared his airway. He started coughing, and his breathing and coloring soon returned to normal.

Angie breathed a sigh of relief as she lay down beside Mikey, while Penny collected all the stuffed animals she could find and placed them on top of him. The next morning, sunlight slanting through the window woke Angie up. Penny was curled up next to Mikey, and they were both sound asleep. Angie thanked God for Penny and for giving her more time with her precious son. Later that year, Penny received the Maui County Hero Award for saving Mikey's life that night.

Mikey's parents noticed that he had fewer seizures since Penny joined their family. Another unexpected benefit of having Penny was that Mikey went outside more often and met many neighbors on their daily walks. Angie enjoyed seeing people's faces light up when they saw Mikey and Penny together. Each day they walked around the edge of Dole Park in the center of town. All the community events took place here, including the annual Easter egg hunt for the island's *keiki* (children).

That spring, Angie and Mike decided to take Mikey and Penny to watch the festivities. The children participated by age groups, with the youngest going first. The girls wore their Easter dresses and the boys had on their Sunday best. Penny sat by Mikey and watched intently as the children raced around the park, hunting for the plastic eggs. One of the organizers came over and asked if Mikey would like to join them, as his age group was coming up next.

It was the first time Mikey had ever been invited to participate in an activity with other children. Angie and Mike thanked him but explained that because of Mikey's vision, he couldn't look for eggs.

"Well, Penny's a retriever; maybe she could help him," the man suggested with a smile.

"That's a great idea. We'd be happy for them to participate!" Angie agreed.

"The next age group is the eight-to-ten-year-olds," the announcer said over the loudspeaker. The children all assembled at the starting line clutching their Easter baskets. Mikey sat in his wheelchair right in the middle, with Penny standing at his side.

"On your mark . . . get set . . . GO!"

Angie unclipped Penny's leash and directed her to "go find." Penny took off with the children, racing around the field looking for the hidden plastic eggs. Mike bumped Mikey's wheelchair across the lawn as Angie ran after Penny as fast as she could. She carried Mikey's Easter basket, which quickly began to fill up. Penny had a unique advantage when it came to finding the hidden eggs because, unlike her competition, she was searching with not only her eyes but also her nose.

A horn blew and the announcer said, "Okay, time's up, everyone! Please bring up your baskets and we'll announce the winner." He held up the first-place prize. It was a huge Easter basket full of assorted goodies. A hush fell over the crowd as they waited to hear who had won.

"This year, in the eight-to-ten-year-old division, the first-place prize goes to . . . Mikey and Penny Raboin!"

Everyone cheered as his parents pushed Mikey's stroller onto the stage and Penny trotted proudly beside him. When

Mikey looked out at the cheering crowd, he started laughing and the crowd cheered even louder. Mikey and Penny remained the reigning champions for the next three years.

When Penny was six years old, the economy slowed down, and Mike lost his job at the hotel. When I asked Angie about their plans, she replied, "We're going to need to move since we're losing our housing too. So we decided to buy an RV on the mainland and travel across the country."

"Really?" I asked in amazement.

"Yes, we're calling it 'Mikey and Penny's Great Adventure'! We want to enjoy the time we have with Mikey and for him to experience as many things as possible. This seems like the perfect opportunity." I was impressed that she could describe losing both their home and income as an opportunity and made a mental note to remember to look for the good in all situations.

They left a month later and sent several postcards from Mikey and Penny's Great Adventure. The first was a picture of the two of them at Disneyland. Mikey and Penny were both wearing Mickey Mouse ears and were posing with none other than Mickey himself. When they finally finished their travels, they settled in California, where they continued to be thankful for each day they had together and lived life to the fullest.

9

Zeus Speaks

Do not ever let what you cannot do interfere with what you can do.

John Wooden

The midday sun beamed down from a cornflower-blue sky as billowy white clouds began to roll in. The Assistance Dogs of Hawaii campus, nestled among the rolling green pastures of Upcountry Maui, was finally complete, and we were celebrating with a traditional Hawaiian blessing. Pastor Tom stood facing the small crowd in the courtyard. His son Mike was one of our first graduates and had a service dog named Quincy. Our other graduates were there too, along with dozens of dedicated volunteers and generous supporters who helped to make this dream a reality.

Will and I stood beside Pastor Tom as he said the blessing and then began a soul-stirring Hawaiian chant. I closed my eyes and listened. The wind suddenly picked up and rustled through the eucalyptus branches high overhead. I thanked God for providing this beautiful property and prayed that it would benefit people on the islands for generations to come.

As Pastor Tom finished his Hawaiian blessing for the new campus, I heard a few gasps and looked up. A bright, double rainbow stretched across the sky above the neighboring pasture. Rainbows appeared here often, but I saw it as a sign and felt God's presence. The clouds grew closer and a gentle mist began to fall. It felt like heaven was reaching down and touching the earth.

I looked through the mist at the ranch-style buildings, painted barn red with white trim, and thought about all the designs Will and I had sketched on scraps of paper and restaurant napkins over the years. There was the state-of-the-art training room we had dreamed about, along with the reception office, classroom, wheelchair-accessible apartments, and exercise yards. The campus was even better than I had ever imagined, and I was overwhelmed with gratitude to have a permanent location. Each day felt like a new adventure filled with endless possibilities.

A week later, I was in Kihei, standing under an awning that sheltered seven yellow Labrador puppies from the sun. I watched as they roughhoused and tumbled on the grass. The puppies were related to Knight, and the breeder had generously offered us the pick of the litter for our program. We'd finally made it all the way through the alphabet and were at the letter Z. I laughed as I watched the puppies clumsily interact with each other and then kneeled to pet them. I noticed one little fellow right away. The puppy with the blue collar sat apart from the others and appeared thoughtful. He stared straight into my eyes and held my gaze with a kind and intelligent expression.

In dog language, prolonged eye contact can be a sign of aggression and is something dogs naturally avoid. Over time, some dogs have become accustomed to our human desire for eye contact. I had a feeling this puppy's focus and good eye contact might be beneficial for his career as a service dog. We performed the temperament evaluations that day, and he had the highest score I'd ever seen. We named him Zeus.

Zeus entered the kindergarten puppy class when he was eight weeks old and was assigned to a puppy raiser named Elaine. She was turning in her previous puppy for advanced training and welcomed Zeus into her home the same day. She started teaching him house manners, social skills, and basic obedience.

Seven months later, Zeus finished the kindergarten and basic training classes and was one of the first dogs to arrive on the new campus for advanced training. I took him on field trips to evaluate his response to environmental distractions such as sight (birds, cats, blowing leaves), sound (cars backfiring), and smell (pretty much everything). Zeus impressed me. Even in public, he had a very high level of handler focus. Zeus was right on track to become a service dog.

We had just hired our first intern, Cate. She was a bright and energetic young woman who had graduated from the Assistance Dog Institute and also had a premed degree. Cate moved into the apartment on campus and helped take care of the growing number of puppies-in-training. She taught Zeus to heel next to both a manual and a power wheelchair. By the time he was twelve months old, Zeus had already mastered over ninety cues.

After eight years of training assistance dogs and seeing all the ways they were making a difference in the world, I felt more inspired than ever. I believed that dogs still had a lot of untapped potential to help people in need, especially in the field of medical bio-detection. I was particularly interested in teaching dogs to detect cancer and other diseases.

I learned about a new graduate degree being offered at Bergin University in California and decided to enroll in the Masters of Science in Canine Studies program. It was a two-year program that required two to three weeks of intensive training at their campus several times a year. The rest of the schooling was online, which would allow me to continue working full-time. I was thrilled to be studying something I was so passionate about and to have the opportunity to learn from some of the top animal behaviorists and dog trainers in the world.

I was surprised by how much more confident I felt going back to school this time. I realized that by spending my time focusing outward and helping others, the fear and anxiety I used to have were gone. In its place was a sense of purpose that gave me a newfound assurance to step outside my comfort zone.

During this time, we received a service dog application from a young man named Brian, who was a graduate student at the University of Hawai'i. Brian had cerebral palsy, a neurological condition that affects muscle tone, movement, and motor skills. Brian used a power wheelchair and was seeking more independence. He was an ideal candidate for a service dog, with one exception: Brian was completely nonverbal. Unfortunately, this made him ineligible to receive a dog, since he wouldn't be able to give the necessary verbal cues. He did qualify for a skilled companion dog, which would require a third member of the team to facilitate the interaction between Brian and his dog. He declined this offer since it wouldn't be feasible for him to have someone following him around all day.

I sat in the classroom in California, listening to a lecture on canine cognition, and couldn't get Brian out of my mind. He was such an intelligent and capable person that I was convinced there must be a way for him to communicate with a dog on his own. I was certain that, by focusing on his abilities rather than his disabilities, we could find a solution. Brian used a text-to-speech device that was attached to the tray on his wheelchair. I wondered if we could record some verbal cues into the device. Perhaps combining those with some simple hand signals would provide a way for him to communicate with a dog.

It came time to choose a subject for my thesis, and I had several ideas in mind. My main focus of study had been cancer detection. However, we were encouraged to think outside the box and come up with something new that hadn't been done before and would also meet an existing need.

I submitted three proposals for my thesis and was thrilled when the committee selected my favorite one! It was creating a new language system for people who are nonverbal to communicate with their service dogs. Brian agreed to partner with me on this project, with a goal of providing him with a service dog he would be able to communicate with directly.

The thought of creating something new to help people with disabilities become more independent was a dream come true. Because of his intelligence and excellent eye contact, I selected Zeus as the dog for Brian. I started off by seeing how Zeus would respond to the recordings. I tried using a text-to-speech device like Brian's and quickly realized this wouldn't work. Tone and timing are two of the most important things in communicating with dogs. Zeus didn't respond well to the monotone computerized voice, and it took far too long to type the cues.

Next, I tried using push buttons that recorded a single word or phrase and that would be attached to his wheelchair. I recorded Will saying a few cues like "sit," "stay," and "come here." This worked better but still wasn't ideal because it was difficult for Brian to reach the buttons due to his limited mobility.

Service Dog Zeus and Brian

After that, we tried a desktop device that had five rows and ten columns of buttons on it. We could record fifty cues in one place! However, this proved difficult because Brian needed his other device on the tray and couldn't switch back and forth. There was also a timing delay in his attempts to push the small buttons. Most importantly, he lost his connection with Zeus by focusing on the device rather than on Zeus. It gradually became clear that recorded cues weren't going to work, so I went back to the drawing board.

I remembered from my days of competing with Bart in AKC obedience trials that communicating with dogs through hand signals worked well. The highest level of training is called "utility" and requires the exclusive use of hand signals when giving instructions to the dogs. Bart had responded well not just to my signals but also to the energy and intent that accompanied them, as well as my facial expressions.

The biggest challenge with using only physical cues was Brian's very limited range of motion. We focused on what he could do rather than what he could not do. He was able to move his head and control his right arm and hand. He could move the fingers on his right hand but not his thumb, which lay at an angle across the palm of his hand. I began creating simple signals using my right arm and hand that Brian would be able to imitate. Zeus quickly learned the signals for "sit" (bending the elbow and bringing the hand up to the shoulder), "down" (pointing the index finger toward the floor), "stay" (extending the arm outward with the palm facing the dog), "shake" (reaching toward the dog with the palm up), "come here" (extending the arm, then bending the elbow and bringing the hand toward the chest), and "let's go" (arm starting at the side and then swinging forward).

I met with Brian and recorded him making all the motions so I could replicate his movements as closely as possible. This would help make it easier for Zeus when it was time for him to transition to working with Brian. When comparing videos of myself and Brian giving the signals, I noticed that, for the "come here" cue, my thumb was pointing upward as I moved my fingers in a beckoning motion toward the palm of my hand.

The next time I practiced "come here" with Zeus, I placed my thumb across my palm (like Brian's) before calling Zeus by bending my fingers. Zeus was sitting all the way across the training room and as soon as I gave the signal, he came immediately. Then, a funny thing happened. The third time I gave the cue, he came as soon as I moved my thumb into position, before I gave the intended signal for "come here." This was the "aha" moment when I realized how tuned in Zeus was to my slightest movements and how much further we could develop this communication system. From then on, I duct-taped my thumb to the palm of my hand before each training session so my signals would look more like Brian's.

I began creating hand signals for all ninety service dog cues and tried to come up with ones that would make sense for both Brian and Zeus. Dogs have a natural instinct to physically synchronize with people. For many signals, my arm represented Zeus's body, and he responded accordingly when I moved it forward or backward or up or down. My hand represented Zeus's head and my fingers represented his mouth. The "hold" cue was simply closing my fist. "Drop it" started with a closed fist, then I opened my hand toward the floor. Zeus was an eager student and rapidly learned all the hand signals. I only needed to give a verbal cue along with a hand signal two or three times before he responded consistently to just the hand signal. Cate knew American Sign Language (ASL), and we incorporated a few of those signs as well.

My biggest concern was how Brian was going to provide feedback to Zeus to help shape his behavior. We came up with a system for this: "good" (a smile), "yes" (a sound from the clicker attached to Brian's armrest) to mark a correct behavior, "that's it" (raised eyebrows and a head nod) to encourage Zeus to keep trying, and "eh" (the sound of a hand slap on Brian's tray) to stop a behavior. I watched videos of Brian and practiced raising my eyebrows, smiling, and nodding my head just like he did.

Once Zeus mastered the individual signals, I tried combining them into sentences, like "Go find Mom." "Go" was pointing away with a finger, and "find" was pointing to my eyes with my peace fingers. "Mom" was a variation of the ASL sign and was a hand beside my face, palm facing forward. The only problem was that whenever I began a sentence with "Go," Zeus went away and didn't see the rest of the signals! I switched the order to put the noun first and verb last, so it became "Mom, find, go." It worked like magic. In a similar way, Zeus learned many things, like "Keys, get, go" and "Door, tug, go."

People were amazed at how well Zeus responded, and visitors to the campus often asked to see "the dog who knew sign language." Guests sat in a row of chairs at the edge of the training room and clapped when Zeus responded to the different signals. He always had extra pep in his step when this happened. Although Zeus was a serious working dog, he was not above appreciating a little applause from the crowd. Zeus enjoyed communicating by sign language so much that if I forgot and gave him a verbal cue by mistake, he would look at me with a blank stare as if to say, *No hablo inglés.*

One day I was in the training room, working on a special request from Brian to teach Zeus to remove a flash drive from a computer. Zeus watched me intently, contemplating the new signal for flash drive. I saw the light of comprehension spark in his eyes, and he went to the computer and carefully removed the flash drive. He looked back at me as he held the small strap in his front teeth. I raised my eyebrows and nodded, just like Brian. Next, I silently signaled "bring it here," "step," and "hand." He stood on the footrests of the wheelchair I was sitting in and placed the flash drive directly into my outstretched palm.

I was astonished by how quickly and easily Zeus learned sign language. It shouldn't have been so surprising, since dogs' primary means of communication is through body language. They communicate with each other this way and are much more adept at reading our body language than we are at reading theirs. What's even more impressive is that dogs learn our spoken language, which is so different from their own. Zeus clearly enjoyed our new way of communicating, and I could tell he appreciated that someone was finally speaking his language.

Speaking his language? I hadn't thought of it in decades but suddenly remembered my birthday wish when I was a little girl. I laughed out loud when I realized that after all these years, my dream had finally come true . . . I WAS TALKING TO ANIMALS!

Brian and his parents came to Maui and attended the first team training camp at our new campus. Not surprisingly, Brian was an excellent student. His father was a kind and soft-spoken man, and his mom was a tiny but mighty lady with a bright smile. They were all quick to see the humor in things and, as usual, I fell in love with not just my client but his entire family.

From the very beginning, Brian had a special connection with Zeus. It occurred to me that both had been trying to communicate without words their entire lives. Now, they had their own language and took it to a whole new level. Zeus watched Brian's face and maintained direct eye contact, just as I'd seen him do as a puppy. He learned every nuance of Brian's expressions and responded to these as well as his hand signals.

We traveled back to Oahu together for the second week of team training camp. The first couple of days, we practiced around their home and neighborhood. Then we went to the UH campus, where Brian was a graduate student and an assistant coach for the football team. He had been a huge football fan since he was a young boy. As an undergraduate, he'd watched the team practice from behind the fence each day after school. A coach noticed him and invited him over to meet the team. They soon discovered that Brian had a great football mind and understanding of the intricacies of the game. He eventually was hired as an assistant coach and helped the UH Warriors achieve their first undefeated season and best national ranking in the school's history.

Brian became an instructor at the University of Hawai'i's College of Education, and Zeus accompanied him to all his lectures. Brian was often seen cruising through the campus in his green UH polo shirt with Zeus trotting next to him. Zeus drew a lot of attention with his good looks and beautiful golden coat. There were distinctive marks on each of his shoulders that were lighter in color than the rest of his coat.

Brian called these his "angel wings" and said they were proof that Zeus was heaven sent.

Zeus was a huge favorite with Brian's students, most of whom were learning to become special education instructors. On the first day of class, Brian demonstrated Zeus's skills by dropping his wallet and having Zeus pick it up and place it in his hand. He shared that he appreciated not having to ask someone for help and joked that he also didn't have to worry about Zeus stealing any money. Brian provided education about service dog etiquette and the importance of not distracting dogs who are working. Much to the delight of his students, Brian always made an exception and allowed them to come up and pet Zeus on the last day of class.

Many of our clients had progressive disabilities, which caused them to lose more mobility and speech over time. I wanted to find a way for them to continue communicating with their dogs when they were no longer able to use their body or voice. I'd learned that just as people do, dogs will follow someone's gaze to see what they're looking at. Based on this, I developed a system of communicating with dogs solely through eye movement called gaze training. I started by teaching the dogs a cue to get their attention (staring directly at them, raising my eyebrows, and blinking twice), which replaced saying their name. Once I had their attention, I gave the next cue, which was glancing quickly at an object, such as a tug rope or light switch, and then back at the dog. The dogs had already learned specific behaviors related to different objects, so they knew what skill to perform when I looked at each one.

When Zeus was seven years old, I was invited to be a presenter at an assistance dog conference in Barcelona, Spain.

Trainers from all over the world attended and shared the latest ideas and innovations. Cate took a break from her doctoral program to meet me there and help give a presentation on the sign language system we had created for Brian and Zeus. Over the years, this incredible team had proven not only that people who are nonverbal can communicate with a dog as well as those who are verbal but that they have the potential to communicate even better. The presentation was well received, and I was thankful to share this information that would help more people who are nonverbal receive service dogs around the world.

Over the years, Brian and Zeus volunteered with our community outreach program and helped students with special needs. Brian also gave motivational speeches at high schools about overcoming adversity and the importance of having a positive attitude. He was a gifted speaker and had an incredible impact on everyone who heard his message. He and Zeus were partners for over twelve years and helped each other to reach their full potential. They remain a shining example of what can be achieved when we choose to focus on our abilities rather than our disabilities.

10

Yoda Brings Hope

Try to be a rainbow in someone else's cloud.

Maya Angelou

I was excited to visit the famous hospital that was so rich in Hawaiian history. The Queen's Medical Center was founded by Queen Emma and her husband, King Kamehameha IV, in 1859 to help care for the Hawaiian people at a time when epidemics were sweeping the islands. It covers twenty acres in downtown Honolulu, with beautiful buildings, sprawling lawns, and huge, old banyan trees.

As we stepped inside the lobby, my senses were overwhelmed by the beauty of the architecture, tropical plants, and paintings that filled the room. The smell of plumeria flowers drifted in through the open windows as an elderly Hawaiian gentleman played the ukulele in the corner. I felt as if I was stepping back in time. Will had stopped and was looking around too.

"What are you thinking about?" I asked as he gazed upward.

"I was wondering why they used that size ductwork for the air-conditioning in here," he replied, as he pointed out the mechanical equipment in the ceiling that I had somehow failed to notice. Will was always one to strike the practical note and never failed to keep my feet a little closer to the ground.

We each held a ten-week-old golden retriever in our arms. The puppies hadn't completed their vaccinations yet, so we had to carry them everywhere because of the risk of parvovirus on the ground. Although Yoda was the smaller of the two, my arms were already getting tired. His coat was baby soft and creamy white in stark contrast to his jet-black nose and pads. His dark eyes looked like they were rimmed with black eyeliner, which made them appear even deeper. Yoda and Yogi were the most docile puppies I'd ever met. I could already picture them working as hospital dogs in the future.

We'd been receiving a growing number of requests for hospital dogs. I appreciated how they could help so many people at a time in their lives when they needed it the most. While service dogs have an incredible depth of impact for one person, the breadth of impact for hospital dogs is truly amazing. On average, they benefit over a thousand patients per year and ten thousand patients during their lifetime.

Our hospital dogs tend to have lower energy than most service dogs and not as much drive. We select dogs who love everyone and enjoy interacting with strangers without being overly solicitous. They also need to be sensitive to people without being overly reactive to their environment. Paula Yoshioka, a vice president of the Queen's Medical Center, heard about the incredible difference Tucker was making at the children's hospital and was interested in applying for a hospital dog of their own. We were on our way to Paula's office to give a presentation to their CEO and other executives.

As we walked down the long hallway, I stared in fascination at the row of royal portraits of Queen Emma and other members of the Hawaiian monarchy. I looked closely at their faces and the expression in their eyes and tried to envision what their lives must have been like. I pictured life in the 1800s and imagined for a moment that I was Emma herself, walking down the same hallway to visit the patients she cared so deeply about. As I turned a corner, I was abruptly brought back to the present when I bumped into a doctor who was looking down at his pager. We both apologized, and when I looked around, I realized Will and Yogi were nowhere to be seen. Yoda looked up at me patiently as I retraced my steps and found Will and Yogi waiting for us by the elevator. Will was laughing.

"I wondered how long it would take you to realize you were going in the wrong direction," he said. "We're going this way; follow me."

I felt a little nervous about giving a presentation to the executives we were about to meet. Yoda and Yogi weren't housebroken yet, and I was hoping they would make it through the presentation without having any accidents. Will liked public speaking even less than I did, so he was mainly there for moral support and to help with the puppies. He jokingly called himself my handler, but it was actually true. Without him I probably wouldn't have even found my way to the hospital.

He carried Yogi in one arm, and a tote bag was slung over his shoulder that contained all the puppies' supplies, as well as my laptop and projector. Everyone's faces lit up as we carried the puppies through the hallways. We found the administrative building and were directed to the executive offices.

"Hi, we're here to see Paula Yoshioka," I said to Barbara, her assistant. She gave a squeal of delight as soon as she saw us, or rather, the puppies.

"It's so nice to meet you. Everyone's been looking forward to your visit," Barbara said.

She led us into the conference room, where there were a dozen people talking quietly around the table. Pandemonium broke loose as soon as they saw the puppies. Barbara introduced us to Paula, who quickly said hello as she reached for Yoda and took him from my arms. She began talking baby talk to him as everyone gathered around her to say hi and pet him. I glanced over at Will, who was laughing and being mobbed by people wanting to pet Yogi. I looked back at Paula, who was now sitting on the floor with Yoda on her lap. He was happily chewing on the hospital name badge that hung from a lanyard around her neck.

"Oh no, I'm so sorry," I exclaimed as I reached for him.

"It's no problem," she laughed. "I'll wear his tooth prints proudly!"

I stood back and watched as their laughter filled the room, and a crowd of people from offices down the hall gathered in the doorway to see what the commotion was. These people made me look like I didn't even like dogs—which wasn't an easy thing to do!

The meeting eventually moved from the floor back to the conference table and Paula proudly introduced Yoda and Yogi to all the staff, who continued to fawn over them. Then she introduced Will and me, and there was considerably less fawning over us.

"Is one of these puppies going to be the dog for Queen's?" a woman asked. The room suddenly went silent as all eyes turned toward me for the first time. Paula's eyes widened with excitement.

"These are just two of several puppies in our training program right now. It's too soon to say what their career paths will be," I replied.

"But . . . is it possible that one of them could be our dog?" Paula pressed.

"Yes, it's possible," I replied and the excitement level in the room rose another notch.

The presentation was a big success and after the meeting, Paula asked if we could take the puppies to the cancer clinic to visit the patients who were receiving chemotherapy. On the way, Paula shared that she had been diagnosed with cancer the year before and had recently finished her treatment.

"I know firsthand how scary it is. Having a dog there would have made such a big difference for me. It's why I'd like to start this program here at Queen's for our cancer patients," she said.

While Will and Yogi visited with nurses in the hallway, Paula and I approached the first station. She drew back the curtain to reveal an elderly Japanese man lying on the bed with an IV taped to his wrinkled arm. His eyes were closed, and it looked like he was in pain.

"Hi, Mr. Kawahara," Paula whispered. He opened his eyes and his brown weathered face broke into a big toothless grin.

"We brought you a special visitor today," she said with a smile. "This is Yoda."

The man's eyes twinkled as he looked at the puppy in my arms. I held Yoda a little closer to the bed so he could reach him.

"Ohhh, he's so soft," he said, as he stroked Yoda's head and gently rubbed one of his velvety ears between his arthritic fingers.

"Would you like him to lie down beside you?" I asked. "He's very gentle."

Paula draped a sheet across the bed, and I laid Yoda gently beside him. Much to Mr. Kawahara's delight, Yoda snuggled in closer and promptly fell asleep.

When it was time to leave, Mr. Kawahara said, "Thank you for bringing him by. You made my day."

"God bless you; we hope you feel better soon." I waved Yoda's paw as we said goodbye and Paula pulled the curtain back. I was impressed with how gentle and careful Yoda had been with him. He looked up at me with his liquid black eyes, and I caught a brief glimpse of what his future would hold.

We visited with a few more patients and it was amazing to see the positive impact the puppies had on each one. They had been such a blessing to so many people and I had a feeling they were already on their way to fulfilling their purpose in life. As Will and I walked back to the parking garage, he took Yoda from me and hoisted him over his shoulder. My arms were tired but my spirit soared.

During the next year, we took Yoda and Yogi on many therapy visits as part of our growing community outreach program. We went to nursing homes, homeless shelters, veterans' agencies, and schools. Yogi loved children and was very outgoing. Yoda was a sensitive soul. He lacked the confidence of some of his classmates but had an affinity for people and a gentleness of spirit that was unique for a puppy. While most of the puppies gravitated toward children, Yoda always preferred visiting the *kupuna*, the respected elders of the Hawaiian community.

He had an unusually solemn expression and people would sometimes ask if he was sad.

"No, that's just Yoda," I'd reassure them. "He's smiling on the inside."

As Yoda entered advanced training, it was clear he lacked the drive and work ethic to become a service dog. He possessed many of the ideal qualities for a hospital dog, but I was concerned that he might be too sensitive for a hospital environment. Then I remembered the cancer clinic at Queen's Medical Center. It was separate from the rest of the hospital and the atmosphere was very quiet and calm, which Yoda would enjoy.

It had been just over a year since our first visit to Queen's. Since then, we'd opened a new office in Honolulu to help meet the growing demand for assistance dogs on Oahu. I called Barbara to ask if I could stop by for a visit with one of our dogs-in-training. The answer to this question was always yes, no matter how busy they all were that day. We arranged to meet Paula at the cancer clinic. Her face lit up when she saw me and the huge, white golden retriever with the jet-black nose at my side. He was unusually serene and had an air of respectability.

"He's gorgeous," she said. "Is this a new one?"

"This is Yoda," I said with a smile. "We brought him last year when he was a puppy."

"He's gotten so big I didn't recognize him!" she said as she knelt down and hugged him.

"How's he doing with his training?" she asked.

"Great! He's almost finished and will be ready to graduate soon."

We walked together into the oncology unit and the receptionists' faces lit up when they saw Yoda. He calmly greeted several people in the waiting room before we went back to the treatment area. The somber heaviness that hung in the air was instantly replaced by joy and laughter with Yoda's presence.

Yoda smiled and slowly wagged his big white tail, fanning it gently from side to side. I watched him closely to see how he felt about the environment. His body language was completely relaxed. He clearly enjoyed interacting with the patients and all the staff. Many of the medical staff remembered Yoda's first visit as a puppy and were delighted to see him again. It takes a special type of person to work in a cancer unit. Yoda seemed like a kindred spirit with them and shared their compassion and kindness. We visited several patients, and many were kupuna. Yoda gave me a rare smile as he snuggled on the bed with one patient and then dozed off while the patient received treatment.

By the end of our visit I felt confident this would be the ideal placement for Yoda. Everyone gathered around to say goodbye as we were getting ready to leave.

"What is Yoda going to do when he graduates?" a nurse asked.

I paused before answering. "I think we might like to place Yoda here with you." The room erupted as Paula hugged Yoda, who wasn't quite sure what all the excitement was about but looked happy nevertheless.

Several staff members applied to be Yoda's handler and caretaker. This was the person who would help facilitate his interactions with the patients and also make sure he got plenty of rest and playtime throughout the day. Yoda would also live with them and be a member of their family. We completed several interviews to find the best match and situation for Yoda. We selected a woman named Pat, who had worked as an oncology nurse for over twenty years. She had lost her own husband to cancer and was very dedicated to the patients she served. Pat was soft-spoken and gentle but had a quiet strength of character and confidence that I knew Yoda would respond well to. When they completed their team training camp, she could hardly wait to get started.

Pat and Yoda shared an office that was right next to the intake area and quickly settled into their daily duties. Yoda's first job was to greet the patients and sit with them while they had their blood pressure taken. He leaned into them as they stroked his soft fur while the nurse pumped the blood pressure cuff. She often had to retake the patients' readings to make sure they were correct. With Yoda by their side, the patients' blood pressure readings were suddenly much lower than ever before. Throughout the day, Pat and Yoda made rounds together and visited with patients while they received chemotherapy. From day one, Yoda provided comfort and courage at a time when the patients needed it the most.

The first patient Yoda visited was a young woman named Grace, who was in her early thirties and had breast cancer. She had been coming to the clinic for radiation and chemotherapy for months. She had lost all her hair and had become increasingly nauseous from the treatment. The week before, she called Pat and told her that she couldn't go on and had decided to

Hospital Dog Yoda and Pat

stop the treatments. Pat told her all about Yoda, who was starting work the following week. The woman was a dog lover, so she agreed to come back one more time, just to meet Yoda.

He calmly lay on the hospital bed by Grace's side during the infusion. She stroked his wavy white coat and petted his long muzzle and soft, floppy ears. Yoda looked at her with a poignant expression, and she said she could feel his healing energy. When the treatment was finished, Pat and Yoda walked her to the front. The receptionist asked if she would like to schedule another appointment.

There was a long pause before she replied, "Yes, but only if Yoda can be there with me." For the next three months, he was the reason she kept coming back. She was eventually cured and gave Yoda credit for being a light she needed in the darkness during that time.

Over the years, many of the hospital staff began stopping by to visit Yoda when they were having a difficult day. He became so popular that the hospital applied for a second dog and received a beautiful yellow lab named Ipo, which means "sweetheart" in Hawaiian. Ipo worked with the patients in the orthopedic and neurology units. The Queen's Medical Center was so thankful for the positive impact the dogs had on their patients that they became major supporters of our program. Their staff even began raising puppies for us as a way to give back. It became commonplace to see a puppy in a blue coat playing in the hallway of the executive offices or snoring under a table during board meetings.

When Yoda was eight years old, I visited the hospital for his annual follow-up visit. I sat with Pat in her office, with Yoda sleeping at our feet, as she talked about Yoda's impact at the hospital.

"You know, it's almost as if I worked in a black-and-white world before. When Yoda arrived, it suddenly became infused with color," she said. "He has brought so much joy and comfort to our patients, their families, our staff, and to me personally. I don't know what we ever did without him."

Later, I followed them on their rounds and watched as Yoda carefully climbed onto the bed and lay next to an elderly Hawaiian woman who was receiving chemotherapy.

"Yoda, you are the best medicine," she whispered in his ear as she slowly stroked his head. "*Tutu* (Grandma) loves you." Her children and grandchildren were visiting from Molokai and took pictures of her with Yoda. They thanked us for bringing Yoda and making their tutu so happy.

As I walked alone through the maze of hallways on my way back to the parking garage, I thought about how many people like Tutu Yoda helped each day. I realized I must have taken a wrong turn when I passed the row of portraits I'd seen on our first visit to the hospital. I stopped at Queen Emma's picture with the ornate gold frame and recalled her mission of helping the Hawaiian people. I looked deep into her eyes . . . and thought I saw her smile. I was grateful to have a small part in continuing her legacy.

11

Pono Finds Justice

*Darkness cannot drive out darkness, only light can
do that. Hate cannot drive out hate, only love can do
that.*

Martin Luther King Jr.

Maisy was born in New Zealand and had the perfect conformation for her breed: a broad head, a barrel chest, an otter tail, and a double coat. She came from top English show lines and had been destined from birth to become a champion, like her parents and grandparents before her. But every time Maisy's breeder led the beautiful black Labrador into the show ring, she plodded slowly around the circle and lacked the spark the judges were looking for.

I had been contacting top breeders around the world looking for puppies to bring to Hawaii for a new type of placement called courthouse dogs. I was disappointed when Maisy's breeder explained she didn't have any puppies available. But when she described how laid back and calm Maisy was, I decided to take a chance. The amiable, two-year-old black Labrador arrived on Maui the following month.

Rule #8: Begin training at eight weeks old.

I picked up Maisy at the airport and she ambled alongside me as we entered the campus. She was immediately engulfed by all the dogs in residence. She rolled onto her back and wagged her tail as she was thoroughly inspected from head to toe. She fit in right away with all the other dogs, who embraced a general philosophy of the more the merrier.

The year before, I had met with the founders of the Courthouse Dogs Foundation when they visited Hawaii. I was hesitant at first because training dogs for this purpose was outside the scope of our mission. Then they explained how children often won't testify in court because they've been threatened, and courthouse dogs help give them the courage to find their voice. I shared this with our board of directors, and they agreed to expand our mission. The victim advocate division of the Honolulu prosecutor's office was our first applicant.

We were going through the alphabet for the second time and were at the letter *P*. We decided to rename Maisy "Pono," which means "righteousness." *Pono* is an important word in the Hawaiian culture and seemed like a fitting name for Hawaii's first courthouse dog.

Pono had such an excellent temperament and pedigree that we decided to breed her once before she graduated so we could carry on her lines. Her puppies were due three days before our annual fundraising gala in February. She was living with Will and me and getting bigger by the day. Will placed the whelping box in our guest room, and Laurie, a dedicated volunteer and experienced puppy nanny, was standing by.

The day of the gala arrived, and the puppies still had not made their appearance. I had just put on my evening gown and was in the bathroom doing my hair and makeup when I heard a shout from the other end of the house.

"Mo, come quick!" Laurie called.

I hitched up my dress and rushed barefoot toward the guest room just in time to see Pono nuzzling her first pup. He had a beautiful black coat and looked just like his mother. My heart swelled as I kneeled to welcome him to our ohana. Will appeared in the doorway, looking dashing in his new navy blazer. He sat down next to me, grinning from ear to ear.

"Look at that big boy," he said, putting his arm around my shoulder. We sat quietly, enjoying the moment, and told Pono what a good girl she was.

Will looked at his watch and said, "We've got to get going."

"Okay, I just need to put on some jewelry. I'll meet you in the car." I was reluctant to leave Pono and her puppy but needed to greet our guests and give a short welcome speech.

We arrived at the Four Seasons Resort just in time. Seeing the gorgeous ballroom filled with all the wonderful people who supported our dream over the years filled me with immense gratitude. Our most generous supporters attended— some even flew in from the mainland for the event. Our regular staff and volunteers ran the entire event, as we didn't have the budget for fundraising staff. Sparkling chandeliers hung from the ceiling, and the koa wood paneling on the walls set off the exotic tropical centerpieces on each table. Festive

Hawaiian music mingled with laughter and friendly chatter. I glanced out at the ocean and saw a pod of humpback whales cruising by. The golden light from the setting sun filled the entire space as Will smiled and squeezed my hand. Everything was perfect. I kept my phone on vibrate as we mingled with guests and thanked them for attending.

Just as the guests were seated in the ballroom, I received a text that another puppy had arrived. A yellow female had joined her brother. I thought it would be fun to update everyone throughout the evening, so I forwarded the pictures Laurie sent to our volunteer who was running the PowerPoint.

Our emcees, Kim and Guy, were popular newscasters and volunteered their services for our event every year. They beamed from behind their podium.

"May I have your attention, please," announced Guy. The conversations quieted as all eyes focused up front.

"It's a girl!" announced Kim, as a picture of a beautiful yellow pup held in the palm of a hand appeared on the huge screen above the stage.

The entire room erupted in applause and cheers. Throughout the evening, Kim and Guy kept everyone updated on Pono's progress and her growing family. When the entrées were cleared, the fundraising portion of the evening began with a "raise the paddle" for donations. By this time, another black female had joined her brother and sister.

The money raised at the annual event provided most of our funding for the year. People sponsored puppies at different levels, which allowed us to place the dogs and provide lifetime follow-up support free of charge. The number of puppies sponsored that night would determine how many puppies we could start in training during the year. When it was time to ask if anyone wanted to sponsor a puppy, paddles were raised all over the room!

At ten p.m., the event concluded, and we said farewell to our guests and volunteers. By then, four puppies had arrived: a black male, a yellow female, and two black females.

When we arrived home, the puppies were all nursing, and Pono was bursting with pride. I was surprised all the puppies hadn't been born yet since the ultrasound had shown six. Laurie was exhausted and I sent her home. I was still wearing my dress, although I'd kicked my shoes off by the door. Will and I knelt next to Pono while she nursed her puppies and patiently waited for nature to take its course. Finally, at midnight, Will turned to me, his eyes red.

"Do you mind if I go to bed?" he yawned. "I've got an early meeting in the morning."

"That's fine; I'm sure it won't be much longer," I assured him as he kissed me good night. "I'll be in soon."

Shortly afterward, Pono began panting nervously and looked agitated.

"What is it, girl?" I asked.

She looked preoccupied and didn't respond. I began to sense that something was wrong. I called the emergency veterinary clinic and explained that it had been two hours since the last puppy was born.

"You'd better bring her right in," the vet said.

"What about her puppies?" I asked in alarm.

"You'll need to bring them too. You can place them in a small box with a hot water bottle and a towel on top. Just make sure they stay warm on the way here."

I was still in my dress as I loaded Pono and the box of puppies into the car. The back seat was folded down and Pono lay on the dog bed in the back. I'd never used the heater in my car before but cranked it up and kept one hand on the puppies to help keep them warm as I gripped the steering wheel with the other and focused on the road ahead.

I pulled into the dark parking lot and the veterinarian came right out and got Pono. I carried the box of puppies inside and sat on a bench with them on my lap in the waiting room. The four tiny puppies were huddled together and made little mewing noises as I petted them to keep them warm. The vet came out about an hour later looking as tired as I felt and even more concerned.

"Pono is doing fine, but I'm afraid we lost a puppy," he said. "There was a large female pup who was stuck in the birth canal and unfortunately didn't make it. The X-ray shows there is another small puppy still inside. We gave Pono a shot, so the pup should be delivered fairly soon. I need to warn you though, it will probably be stillborn considering its size and the amount of time that has passed."

It was three a.m. as I drove home, exhausted. Pono lay on her bed in the back of my SUV and the pups slept beside me with a newly filled hot water bottle in the bottom of their box. I heard a noise in the back and turned on the overhead light. Pono was moving around and seemed uncomfortable.

"Oh no, please not now," I whispered as I pulled the car over on the shoulder of the deserted highway.

I parked the car and climbed into the back with Pono. She had already broken the sac and was vigorously licking a tiny black puppy, who was half the size of the others. His lifeless little body flopped back and forth, and my eyes filled with tears as I watched Pono's desperate attempts to revive him.

"Good girl, Pono," I whispered. "It's okay. You're such a good girl."

I couldn't bear to watch any longer. I closed my eyes and said a prayer. Suddenly, I heard a tiny squeak and my eyes opened wide. The puppy's little body was moving slightly. Pono glanced at me, and I saw a look of profound relief on her face. She gently nudged him toward her belly, but he wasn't strong enough to nurse. I picked him up and squeezed the teat to start some milk flowing. His body felt lifeless in my hand as I placed his mouth directly over the nipple. His mouth didn't close, and his head drooped to the side. I held it up and tried again. This time his mouth closed, and he slowly started to nurse. Soon he was latched on and doing a head bob, while his little feet pumped back and forth on either side. Pono and I looked at each other and shared a moment of intense relief and love for this tiny being.

As I pulled into our driveway, dawn was beginning to break, and an orange glow was spreading above Haleakala. Not being much of a morning person, this was a rare sight for me. I took a moment to appreciate the beautiful dawn of a new day and thanked God for the five new lives he had blessed us with and said a prayer for the precious one we had lost.

I woke up around noon and went to check on the puppies. Will was leaning over the whelping box, and I could tell by the look on his face that something was wrong.

"What is it?" I asked.

"I think there's something wrong with the little one's leg."

I looked in the whelping box and could easily spot the last puppy born since he was so much smaller than the rest. His back left leg was limp and dragging behind him as he crawled toward Pono.

Will called our veterinarian, and she came over that afternoon. "The circulation to his leg must have been cut off during the delivery," she said, shaking her head. "I'm afraid it will need to be amputated as soon as he is old enough."

Pono was a solicitous mother and took excellent care of her puppies. She was extra doting on the little one, as we all were. He was such a happy and brave pup that we decided to name him Soldier in honor of his courageous spirit. He had surgery when he was just three weeks old, and the vet suggested that he wear a cotton onesie to help keep the bandages in place. So, in addition to being the smallest and missing a leg, he was now wearing tiny pajamas. This of course made him irresistible to everyone who met him, and Soldier was delighted with all the extra attention.

Two months later, Pono's maternity leave was ending, and it was time for her to begin her career as a courthouse dog. Everyone at the Honolulu prosecutor's office had been eagerly awaiting her arrival so they could finally meet her in person. There was one small complication though: Pono had yet to get her girlish figure back.

Donna and I sat in the reception office on campus discussing the upcoming meeting when Pono walked by us. We stared together in silence. Her mammary glands were almost touching the floor and swayed tremendously back and forth as she walked. When she sat down, they somehow looked even more prominent as they stacked on top of each other in huge layers.

"I don't think I should take her to Honolulu looking like this," I said in despair. "And our meeting at the prosecutor's office is in just a few days."

"It does look rather shocking, especially when she sits down and lets it all hang out." Donna laughed. "But I have an idea that might work. Don't postpone your trip yet!"

The next morning, Donna showed up at the office and produced a garment out of her purse, like a magician pulling a rabbit out of a hat.

"Ta-da!" she said.

"What is it?" I asked, looking at the piece of black material.

"It's doggy shapewear," she announced proudly. "I made it out of a cotton tube top."

She called Pono and slipped it over her head. Pono smiled obligingly as Donna stretched it across her sagging midsection, tucking everything in as she went.

"When you put her blue assistance dog coat over it, no one will even know it's there, because it blends in with her black fur," Donna said. I couldn't believe my eyes; it was like magic! Pono had her girlish figure back in an instant.

The following week, Pono and I were in downtown Honolulu and had just parked in front of the Iolani Palace. The majestic building is the only royal palace in the United States and is surrounded by manicured lawns and forbidding gates. Seeing it, I felt the familiar tug of the past and those who had come before. Time rolled away as I looked at the upstairs window where Queen Liliuokalani had been imprisoned during the overthrow of the Hawaiian monarchy. I pictured her sitting at her desk and looking out the window as she wrote her memoirs.

Pono's wet nose on my arm brought me back to the present. We crossed the street to the high-rise building that housed the prosecutor's office. Before entering, I glanced furtively around and, when no one was watching, slipped the black shapewear over Pono's head and then put on her blue Assistance Dogs of Hawaii coat. I smiled in triumph at her suddenly svelte figure as we entered the imposing-looking building.

We took the elevator up to the top floor and walked through a maze of hallways to the chief prosecutor's office. The secretary greeted me and said, "I'll let him know that you're here."

He arrived a few minutes later and greeted me as he beamed down at Pono.

Within minutes we were surrounded by dozens of attorneys and other staff who had come out to meet Pono.

"This is our new courthouse dog, Pono," the prosecutor proudly proclaimed to the crowd who had circled around us. Pono heard her name and smiled up at him and wagged her tail. Then she sat down. Everyone stopped talking and stared at Pono with their mouths hanging open. Unfortunately, when she sat down, the top of her undergarment rolled down a few inches, and her top two boobies were now peeking out in the most eye-popping way. I stood frozen, as all eyes turned toward me. I attempted to laugh as I reached down and pulled up her top.

"Well, you see, she had puppies recently and hasn't quite gotten her figure back yet," I faltered as one of her teats popped back out.

"Pono, down," I pleaded. She lay down and smiled up at everyone with such a joyful expression that everyone quickly recovered their composure and ignored her unfortunate wardrobe malfunction.

A month later, Pono began team training camp with her new partner, Dennis, who was the director of the victim advocacy division and had worked at the prosecutor's office for over thirty years. Although admittedly not a dog person, he was committed to doing everything he could to help victims. He was quick to recognize the value of having a dog available for children during forensic interviews, medical exams, and even while testifying in court.

Dennis was a kindhearted, affable man, and he and Pono formed an instant friendship during team training camp. Dennis had never had a dog, so he was starting from scratch. He learned all the basic cues and then progressed to specialized skills that he would use to have Pono interact with children, such as "visit" and "snuggle." They practiced walking through crowded hallways and doing long "down-stays" in the witness stand so she would be ready for the courtroom.

From the first day, it was evident that Pono's maternal instincts carried over from her puppies to the keiki she worked with. She was so nurturing and loved snuggling up with them

Courthouse Dog Pono and Dennis

on the couch in the interview room. An important part of her job was to provide comfort and courage to children during forensic interviews, which could last for a couple of hours. Pono was also present during medical exams. When cases went to trial, she accompanied the child to the witness stand and lay silently at their feet while they testified. Pono was always steady and predictable, which was crucial since a mistrial could be declared if she did anything to disrupt the proceedings. More than anything, Pono helped children find their voice.

Pono was so successful at helping children testify that a cold case was reopened in hopes that she would be able to help the victim talk and justice would finally be found.

"It's the worst case of child abuse I've seen in thirty years," Dennis said. "The fact that we couldn't get a conviction still keeps me up at night."

The twelve-year-old girl was told about Pono and agreed to come back one more time. She arrived with her foster parents, who waited in the lobby while she was escorted into the interview room. The room was small and sparsely furnished, with a one-way mirror on one of the walls, which detectives sat behind. There was a small couch against the opposite wall, and the girl slipped off her shoes and sat on it with her feet curled under her. She took a deep breath and tightened her ponytail.

Dennis arrived and introduced himself and Pono.

"Would you like her to sit with you?" he asked with a smile. The girl kept her eyes on Pono, who looked up at her and slowly wagged her tail. She nodded and gave a small smile. Pono saw the sadness in the girl's eyes and sensed her pain. "Jump on," Dennis said, and Pono hopped up on the couch and curled up next to her, gently resting her big black head across the girl's lap. The interviewer came in and quietly took a seat.

"She's so sweet," the girl whispered as she traced her fingers across the noble outline of Pono's head. Pono soon fell fast asleep, and the rising and falling of her chest and steady breathing had a calming influence on everyone in the room. The girl stroked Pono's back and began to talk. After about an hour, they finally asked the most important question, the one that could lead to a conviction. She stopped talking.

"I can't tell you that," she finally whispered as tears spilled down her cheek and dropped onto Pono. Dennis and the interviewer were skilled at hiding their emotion, so their disappointment didn't show. They had been waiting years for justice to be served and they were so close. They watched in silence for a few minutes as the girl petted Pono's face. Then she looked up at them and said, "But I will tell her."

She left Pono lying on the couch and slid to the floor. She turned her back to the interviewers and held Pono's face in her hands. She looked deep into her tranquil eyes and knew she had finally found someone she could trust. When she finished talking, the prosecutors had all the information they needed to put the perpetrator behind bars and make sure the atrocities would never be repeated.

"Goodbye, Pono," she whispered as she wrapped her arms around Pono's neck and buried her face in her fur. "Thank you."

Dennis and Pono were an incredible team and over the years helped hundreds of the most vulnerable members of the community find their voice. Pono also provided support for her coworkers. Dennis scheduled a Pono "happy hour" each afternoon where staff could play and interact with Pono as a means of stress relief. The grim reality is that prosecuting criminals is not an easy job, and I developed a profound respect for all the people who work behind the scenes to keep the rest of us safe. The success of Dennis and Pono's partnership and groundbreaking work opened the door for courthouse dogs to be placed on all the islands. Thanks to Pono, Hawaii soon became the first state in the country to have a courthouse dog in every jurisdiction.

12

Emma to the Rescue

Hardships often prepare ordinary people for an extraordinary destiny.

C. S. Lewis

Rich was an impressive waterman. On any given day, he could be found paddling out to find the perfect wave, his bright smile flashing as he navigated the watery terrain. Whether it was surfing or kayaking, or even competing internationally in tennis tournaments, Rich lived a full and active life. He was well-known in the community and worked for the Department of Parks and Recreation helping people with disabilities enjoy the outdoors. He inspired everyone around him to embrace life with courage and optimism. But Rich didn't just talk about overcoming challenges, he lived it. Rich was a paraplegic.

When Rich was fourteen years old, he was walking home from school with his younger sister and girlfriend. A drunk driver swerved off the road, plowing directly into them. Rich survived but was paralyzed from the waist down. Tragically, his sister and girlfriend both lost their lives in the accident. While Rich was in the hospital, he made a decision that he was not going to live the rest of his life as a victim. With God's help, he forgave the driver of the car. He decided that in memory of his sister and girlfriend he was going to live life to the fullest and help other people with disabilities do the same.

Rich became a top wheelchair athlete and spent several years traveling around the world competing in wheelchair tennis tournaments before returning home to Honolulu and helping to start a nonprofit organization called AccesSurf. Its mission is to encourage people with disabilities to enjoy the ocean and water sports.

Rich called our office one day, wanting to find out more about service dogs.

"I've been super active all my life," he said. "I've thought about getting a service dog for a while but am worried a dog might slow me down. I'll need one who can keep up with me."

I smiled and looked at the big yellow lab across the room. Emma seemed to know something was up and thumped her tail enthusiastically.

"Rich," I replied, "it's possible we might have just the dog for you."

Emma was a happy and confident dog, with a bit more energy than most. She had a very strong work ethic, but her most attractive quality was her enthusiasm. She was eager to please and was always game to try anything that I asked of her. She loved to work and although she was ready to graduate, there hadn't been anyone on the waiting list who was active enough for her . . . until now!

Team training camp was quickly approaching and it sounded like Rich might be an ideal match for Emma, who would appreciate his active lifestyle.

We expedited Rich's application, and the documents confirmed what I had suspected—it was a match made in heaven! Just to be safe, I wanted Emma to meet Rich so I could see how they interacted before making a final decision. Dogs clearly convey through their facial expressions and body language how they feel about the people they meet.

I arranged to meet Rich at the Kahala Mall before going to his house for the home interview. Just minutes from Waikiki and within sight of Diamond Head, the mall was filled with crowds of locals and tourists. My stomach growled as Emma and I headed for Whole Foods. I looked forward to having lunch with Rich and getting to know him a little better.

I spotted Rich right away. He was sitting alone at an outside table, and when he saw us, he waved, and his face lit up with a huge smile. As we got closer, Emma pulled toward him, like she was greeting an old friend. Before I could stop her, she put her paws on his lap and kissed his face. I was relieved to see that Rich enjoyed her exuberant greeting. He laughed with delight and hugged Emma—it was love at first sight!

Neither could stop smiling or take their eyes off each other throughout the lunch. I felt a little like a third wheel and was tempted to hand her over right then and there. Instead, Emma and I followed Rich to his house in Hawaii Kai for the home interview. We drove along the rugged coastline before turning up into the verdant valleys of Hawaii Kai.

Rich wheeled up the ramp and held the door open for us. It was a lovely one-story home that had been remodeled to be wheelchair accessible. Like Rich, the house had a cool surfer vibe. There were wooden surfboards hanging on the wall in the living room and a guitar in the corner.

Emma slept under his kitchen table with her head on his footrest while I asked Rich about the specific ways a dog could assist him.

"I live alone and when I drop things, I have a hard time picking them up off the floor," he said. "Sometimes when I'm in bed, my wheelchair rolls away and I'm not able to reach it." I quickly scribbled on my notepad as he spoke. "I could also use help with opening and closing doors, turning on and off lights, and maybe getting a drink from the refrigerator. It would be awesome to have someone like Emma who could help me around the house."

Rich's spinal cord injury was on his lower spine, so he was able to use a manual wheelchair. However, pushing a wheelchair for so many years was hard on his shoulders and had required surgery. He wanted a dog who could be taught to help pull his wheelchair when he had to travel long distances.

"I also like to go to the beach every day and get in the ocean," he said. "I do okay getting down to the water's edge but when I get out of the water, it's hard to scoot uphill and pull my wheelchair with me. Do you think a dog would be able to help pull my wheelchair across the sand back to the parking lot?"

I thought about this for a minute before answering. "Tug" was the only skill Emma wasn't very proficient at. Despite her athleticism, she tugged quite daintily and could barely pull open a drawer. However, in the final stage of training, I always like to take the dog's weakest area and make it a strength.

"Yes, I think she could learn to do that," I replied. He showed me where a tug rope could be fastened to his wheelchair and I took some pictures so Will could simulate this back on campus. I could hardly wait to get back to Maui and start teaching Emma this helpful new skill.

Rich asked if Emma would like to swim in his pool and was delighted when I said yes. He opened the sliding doors from the kitchen that led to a small lanai and a swimming pool that took up most of the yard.

It was a hot and humid afternoon, and I wished I could join her but hadn't brought my swimsuit. Rich threw a tennis ball in the middle of the pool and laughed out loud as Emma leaped after it and caught it in the air. His blue eyes twinkled, and his whole face lit up as he watched her swim. Emma seemed so at home with Rich and was reluctant to leave when it was time for us to go. As we drove away, she looked out the back window at Rich, who was waving goodbye to her from his driveway.

Back on Maui, I worked with Emma around the campus teaching her how to pull me in a manual wheelchair. She quickly learned how to pull fast and slow, left and right, and to stop on cue.

On the weekends, Will and I trained Emma at the beach by our house. It was challenging to pull a wheelchair through deep sand, so we started by teaching her how to pull it across a flat lawn. Emma loved tennis balls, so we attached one to the Velcro strap on a boogie board leash and taught her to pull the board across the lawn by holding on to the tennis ball. She loved this, so we transferred the boogie board leash and tennis ball to the wheelchair, and she learned to pull it too. Next, she pulled the wheelchair across a lawn that

Service Dog Emma and Rich

was slightly uphill, then we moved to the beach. She pulled the chair across the hard-packed sand near the water's edge, where it was easier for the wheels to roll. After that, she learned to pull the chair across the soft sand, where she had to really put her weight into it. The last step was having her pull the wheelchair uphill through the soft sand. It took all her strength, but she loved doing it, especially because people on the beach often watched and cheered her on. Emma was a bit of a show-off!

Rich asked if Emma could learn to do water rescue in case he ever needed help when he was out in the ocean. Will taught Emma to swim right next to him and wear a life jacket with a handle that he could hold on to. While they were swimming, Will said, "Go to shore!" At the same time, I called her from the beach. He held on to the handle and she towed him to shore. Soon she responded to just his cue.

We also taught her to rescue someone on a surfboard or kayak by holding a strap in her mouth and pulling them to shore. I would sit on my board out past the shore break and call, "Emma, help!" as I waved my arms. Will let her go and she immediately charged through the surf, swam to me, and grabbed the strap with her mouth. Then, I lay down on the board and said, "Go to shore," and she towed me all the way back to shore. Beachgoers cheered her on, and this soon became her favorite thing to do.

One morning, Will and I were standing at the water's edge with Emma and talking to friends. There was a woman in a tiny bikini doing yoga on her paddleboard just offshore. One of her poses involved reaching her arms overhead. Unfortunately, this looked a little too much like the signal for help. Emma was eager to assist and charged into the ocean at full speed. I ran almost as fast and dove into the water right after her, but Emma was a much faster swimmer. I watched in horror as she grabbed the paddleboard's strap that was floating in the water and began towing the paddleboard to shore. The unsuspecting woman was doing a downward-dog pose and hadn't noticed her board was moving yet. I called out, "Emma, drop it," as sternly as I could, but she was determined to complete her mission of mercy. As they got close to shore, a wave knocked the woman off her board. Emma dropped the strap and returned to shore, looking extremely pleased with herself. I apologized profusely to the woman and hoped she might see the humor in the situation. She did not . . . but everyone on the beach did!

Rich attended team training camp on Maui with two other gentlemen who were also receiving service dogs. One had multiple sclerosis, and the other had ALS. We practiced around the campus and at the shopping mall in town during the first week. The second week of training took place on Oahu, where we practiced Emma's skills at home and out in public. She loved pulling Rich in his wheelchair, especially at Costco, where his mom worked. Rich and Emma both had huge smiles as they whizzed down the wide aisles together.

During his first follow-up visit, Rich reported that Emma went everywhere with him and was always eager to help. They loved going to the beach every day, and her favorite activity was kayaking with Rich. She wore a bright orange life jacket and Rich would grab its handle and pull her up onto the two-person kayak. She sat proudly in the front seat, occasionally leaning over to watch the fish, while Rich sat in the back and paddled. Emma became a pro at pulling Rich's wheelchair from the water's edge and across the sand, up to the parking area. They were featured in a commercial for Assistance Dogs of Hawaii, and Rich is still asked from time to time if Emma is "the dog from that commercial."

We often have graduate reunions, where our ohana gets together just for fun. It's heartwarming to see old friends reconnect—both human and canine. The dogs who had been classmates are always so excited to see each other again and pair off and play together.

Rich hosted several pool parties at his house. All our graduate teams on Oahu attended. We played lots of games and had prizes for the dog who jumped the farthest into the pool and swam the fastest. There was even a relay race, where two teams of dogs competed. Each dog swam two lengths of the pool before their teammate jumped in. The dogs tended to get overly enthusiastic during the relay race. The ones in line didn't always wait their turn before jumping in, which caused frequent disqualifications and general mayhem. Emma was very competitive, especially when it came to the farthest jump contest. We all looked forward to watching her defend her title each year against Pono, who was often a close runner-up.

Rich was already independent before he received Emma, but he shared how she had made his life much easier and infinitely happier than when he was alone.

"Emma is always aware of my every thought, movement, and feeling," Rich told me during a follow-up visit. "She is right beside me and ready to help if I forget something, drop something, or am just having a difficult day. She is for sure my best friend."

One year, guests at the annual pool party included two of our newest graduates, a hospital dog team named Katie and Angel. Katie was a lovely recreational therapist who worked with Angel at a rehab hospital and had a son named Cameron. Angel and Emma enjoyed playing together, so Rich invited Katie to bring Angel back for a playdate. Soon, the dogs weren't the only ones dating. Rich and Katie fell in love and eventually got married. Much to their delight, Emma and Angel became sisters and got to play together every day. Two years later, their family welcomed another little sister to their family . . . this one with two legs!

13

Bailey Goes to Japan

*We can do no great things; only small things with great
love.*

Mother Teresa

The two puppies happily tumbled out of their shared crate
looking like fluffy polar bear cubs with their matching snow-
white coats and coal-black noses. Bailey and his sister, Bella,
were just ten weeks old. They came from a breeder in Mel-
bourne, who was world renowned for her champion English
cream golden retrievers. Bailey was much larger than his sister. He had a broad head, huge paws, and shiny black eyes that
suggested a kind and gentle soul.

"I think I'm in love," said Sharon, one of our puppy raisers, as she picked up Bailey and held him in her arms. Bailey
looked up at her and smiled and wagged his tail as if to say,
Me too! Earlier that year, Sharon's son Scott had volunteered

at our campus as part of a school project. After much persuading, Sharon's husband, Ron, finally agreed to give puppy raising a try. Sharon loaded the kennel in the back of her car, and Bailey sat on Scott's lap as they drove home. Of course, once they arrived home, Ron immediately fell in love with Bailey too.

From the beginning, Bailey had a special relationship with Scott, who was twelve years old and had recently been diagnosed with Crohn's disease. Whenever Scott was in pain, Bailey kept him company and snuggled with him. Bailey's warm body acted like a heating pad and he licked away the tears from Scott's cheeks. Sharon and Ron were surprised by Bailey's compassion and how in tune he was with Scott, especially when Scott was in pain. Bailey was still just a puppy, so it was far too soon to choose his career path. I couldn't help but notice that he had the ideal temperament for a hospital dog, which gave me high hopes for his future.

Bailey was five months old and attending puppy class at our campus when he had his first seizure. We rushed him to the vet and the convulsions stopped by the time we arrived. The vet explained this sometimes happened once and then never again. Unfortunately, a week later Sharon reported that Bailey had another seizure and this one lasted even longer. He was diagnosed with epilepsy and prescribed seizure medication for the rest of his life. The medicine made Bailey lethargic and the light was suddenly gone from his eyes. Assistance dogs have to pass rigorous health screening and can't have any major health issues, so we released Bailey from the program. We had a long waiting list of people hoping to adopt our "career-change" dogs, and we placed him with a volunteer named Jennifer, who was a pediatrician.

When Bailey had just turned a year old, Jennifer called to let us know how well he was doing. She explained that children sometimes have seizures as their brains are developing and then never have one again. So, after a period with no seizures, she had taken Bailey off his medicine, and he hadn't had another one since.

"That's wonderful news! I'm happy to hear that he's doing so well," I said, feeling a huge sense of relief.

"I've been bringing him to my office a couple days a week, and he's been incredible with my patients." She paused and then added, "He's such an amazing dog, I really think he would do well as a full-time hospital dog. I'd like to offer him back to you so he can help more children."

"Oh, Jennifer, are you sure?"

"Yes, I'm going to miss him, but I think it's what he was born to do."

I was touched by her selflessness. So many people make sacrifices for each one of our dogs to help others that I often feel like I'm surrounded by heroes. Volunteers welcome the puppies into their hearts and homes knowing they will one day give them up. Sponsors make a financial sacrifice that allows us to place the dogs and provide lifetime follow-up support free of charge. Countless other volunteers, donors, and board members generously offer their time and resources in hopes of making a positive difference in someone else's life. They say it takes a village to raise a child, but it's also true that it takes a village to raise an assistance dog.

Bailey came back to campus and rejoined his classmates, who were thrilled to see their old friend again. He had grown into a beautiful and regal-looking dog, with his long, white coat and perfect conformation. He quickly caught up on his lessons and joined the advanced training class for hospital dogs. His favorite thing to do was "snuggle," where he carefully lay next to someone and gently rested his big head across them. Despite his large size, Bailey had excellent body awareness and was very careful around splints, bandages, and the IV tubes that were part of the required training for hospital dogs. Bailey was almost ready to graduate, but we didn't have any hospitals on the waiting list. I waited and wondered where he was going to be placed.

I didn't have to wait long. I received an email from a woman named Kim Forsythe in Japan. She and her husband had recently started Shine On! Kids in memory of their son Tyler, who had died of complications from leukemia treatment when he was just two years old. He was diagnosed at one month old and had spent almost his entire life in the hospital.

She explained that the Japanese government supported 100 percent of medical costs for very sick children. She was so grateful for the care Tyler received that she wanted to give back and help others.

Kim's organization, Shine On! Kids, supported Japanese children and their families who were experiencing challenges due to medical difficulties. Although there were many organizations like this in the United States, there was no one serving families this way in Japan.

Kim had heard about the positive impact Tucker was having on the patients at the children's hospital on Oahu and traveled there to find out more about the program. After meeting Tucker and hearing such great reports about how he helped children heal, she was determined to start a similar program in Japan.

My heart went out to her and I really wanted to help, but our mission statement said we only placed dogs in Hawaii. I told her I was sorry and gave her the contact information for some programs in Japan and Australia. She called back two days later and said the other programs did not train hospital dogs, and she really wanted a dog from us.

There were lots of reasons to say no. The logistics for placing a dog internationally were complicated. Not only that, I was also concerned that if we expanded outside of Hawaii, we might lose support from some donors and end up helping fewer people in the long run.

However, one rule I try to live by is not to allow the fear of something bad to ever prevent me from doing something good. I thought about how many thousands of sick children a dog could help and how this placement could open the door for more hospital dogs in Japan and throughout Asia. How could I say no to that?

I asked our dear friend Mary, who was our biggest supporter and had shared our vision from the beginning, what she thought about the placement.

"Why not?" she replied in her usual practical manner. "What does it matter where they live if a dog can help children with cancer?"

I gave her a hug and thanked her for confirming my decision. The board agreed to expand our mission to allow placements outside of Hawaii on a case-by-case basis.

Rule #9: ~~Place dogs only in Hawaii.~~

I called Kim to tell her the good news, and she submitted their completed application the same day. She wanted a dog for the Shizuoka Children's Hospital, where her son had been a patient. She explained that they had very strict infection control policies. Once the children were diagnosed with cancer, they usually stayed in the hospital, even between treatments, which could take years. Parents were allowed daily visits, as long as they wore a mask, but young siblings were not allowed to visit.

"Are you sure they will allow a dog in the hospital?" I asked.

"I've been meeting with the director and the board, and we should have approval soon," she replied. I knew firsthand that Kim was a hard person to say no to. I was counting on her optimism and determination to overcome any obstacles the hospital administration might present.

To help with Bailey's training, Shine On! Kids translated the ninety cues from English to Japanese. Thankfully, I had studied Japanese for a year in college and had a basic understanding of the language and pronunciation. It was humbling to realize that Bailey still learned the Japanese words much faster than I did. Before our training sessions each day, I wrote the cues on my arm so he wouldn't have to wait while I stopped and looked at the list.

"*Ikimasho* (Let's go)," I said as we started walking. "*Osuwari* (Sit)," I told him as we stopped. Dogs don't hear languages, just sounds. They also respond much more to the tone than the actual words we say. Bailey soon learned all ninety cues in Japanese and became our first bilingual dog. (Except, of course, for Zeus, who knew sign language!) We completed Bailey's training on Oahu so he could shadow Tucker at the children's hospital. One of the most effective ways dogs learn is by watching each other, and Bailey learned from the best.

It's as important to choose the right person for a hospital dog team as it is to choose the right dog. Kim decided that Bailey's handler should be a pediatric nurse. Although the handler wouldn't have specific nursing duties, that background would help them to interact with patients and communicate with staff. Kim interviewed several pediatric nurses to find the ideal handler for Bailey. She asked me to interview the top three candidates and make a decision. The interviews were conducted online with the help of an interpreter.

My favorite applicant was Yuko, a lovely pediatric nurse in her late twenties. She was polite and professional and, like most people who work in children's hospitals, also very kind. She was eager to embrace this opportunity and was looking forward to starting work.

I believed that Yuko would not only interact well with children but would also be a strong advocate for the new program in Japan. Most important, she appeared to be the perfect match for Bailey. Thanks to Shine On! Kids' support, Japan became the first country to have a full-time paid position for a hospital dog handler. They also provided an apartment for Yuko and a car to transport Bailey to and from work.

Yuko arrived on Maui for team training camp, accompanied by the manager of Shine On! Kids and an interpreter. I was relieved to see that she and Bailey immediately hit it off since this was the first time a team hadn't met before the team training camp. Between training sessions, I noticed her gently petting Bailey and speaking softly to him, which he adored. We completed the first week of training at the Maui campus and then traveled to Oahu to practice for several days with Hospital Dog Tucker and his handler, Dr. Wendi, at Kapiolani Medical Center.

It almost took an act of Congress for Bailey to travel to Japan due to their strict policies for dogs entering the country.

However, Kim was a woman who made things happen and once again I appreciated her can-do attitude. She arranged for Bailey to travel to Japan with Yuko, so he could settle into his new home before I arrived for the final week of training.

I dropped Yuko and Bailey off at the international gate at the Honolulu airport. As I stood at the curb and watched them walk away, I idly wondered what dogs must think about airplanes. They must find it surprising to board the plane somewhere familiar and hours later step off the same plane into a completely different world. One with different smells, sounds, and sights, where the people, animals, and plants all look different. Dogs have no concept of the distance planes travel, and I imagined it must seem to them like the train station in the Harry Potter novels, where they are magically transported to a strange new world.

My meditations were interrupted by the sound of the security guard's voice. "Ma'am, you'll need to move your car."

I gave Yuko and Bailey a final wave before I hopped into my car and drove away.

I had a lot of work to do before I joined them two weeks later in Japan to complete their training at Shizuoka Children's Hospital. Kim warned me there was still some reluctance to the idea among the medical staff and asked me to prepare a PowerPoint presentation for the hospital. I wanted to deliver a convincing argument for the hospital dog program, so I included all the evidence-based research I could find on the various health benefits Bailey could provide for their patients with cancer and other diseases. I completed the presentation and Kim had everything translated to Japanese.

Will was finishing a building project and planned to meet me in Shizuoka at the end of the week. I'm not sure which one of us was more concerned about me traveling alone to a foreign country. He drove me to the airport and quizzed me along the way.

"Are you sure you've got your boarding pass?"

"Yep."

"ID?"

"It's right here."

"Cell phone?"

"Check!"

"Do you have the contact number for your translator?"

"It's already in my phone!"

"Don't forget your backpack."

"Don't worry; I'll be fine!"

"Okay," he said with a smile. "I'll be praying for you and will see you on Friday."

We kissed goodbye at the curb, and I made my way toward international departures.

Twelve hours later, I stepped off the plane at the Narita Airport. Although the crowds and frenetic pace were different from anything I'd ever seen, everyone was very polite, and I felt completely safe. My interpreter was waiting for me at the baggage claim area, holding a sign with my name on it. She was a young woman named Kana who had attended college in Chicago. I followed her around like a puppy dog as we went through the airport, transferred trains, and eventually arrived in Shizuoka just before dark. We had a quick bite to eat, and I'm still not sure what it was. When I finally arrived at the hotel, I tottered into the small room and collapsed on the bed.

I woke up to the sound of my alarm the next morning, and Kana met me in the lobby to take me to the hospital for the early morning presentation. Kim met us in the auditorium and introduced me to some of the medical staff before we began. I didn't need an interpreter to see that several were not in favor of this idea. The look on their faces said it all. I had gotten a little better at public speaking over the years but still felt nervous. As I walked on the stage with Kana, she reminded me to pause after a few sentences to give her time to translate. She also reminded me that most of the two hundred staff members in the audience would not understand what I was saying, which was somehow reassuring.

With my heart pounding, I approached the microphone and began.

"*Ohayōgozaimasu. Yonde kurete arigatō* (Good morning. Thank you for having me here)," I said, before switching to English.

The presentation took about an hour, and it was difficult to judge the reaction of the audience while I was speaking. At the end, everyone smiled and applauded enthusiastically.

The next day, Kim said that the presentation had been a big success and we had been given permission to take Bailey to the hospital on Mondays, Wednesdays, and Fridays from nine to eleven a.m. I was surprised by the time restriction, but she assured me that if all went well, they would increase the amount of time. Then she said that Bailey was not allowed to go in the hospital rooms, only the hallways. I tried to hide my disappointment but began to wonder if all the hard work and specialized training was worth it if this was all he was allowed to do.

Yuko, Kana, and I arrived with Bailey at the hospital early the next morning. I was surprised to see some familiar faces on the wall in the lobby. Not only were there pictures of Bailey

Courtesy of Shine On! Kids

Hospital Dog Bailey and patient

as a puppy, there were also pictures of his puppy raisers: Ron, Sharon, and Scott.

We were given surgical masks and gowns to wear before entering the first unit. Bailey stood patiently at Yuko's side as a nurse pushed a button on the wall and the heavy metal doors slowly swung open. The hall was so crowded we could hardly walk through. The nurse explained that when the parents found out Bailey wouldn't be allowed in the rooms, they had pushed their children's beds into the hallway to see him! After that, Bailey was allowed to go into the patients' rooms.

Two days later, I was making rounds with Yuko and Bailey when we were asked to visit a patient in room 317. We entered the room and saw a woman standing next to her young son's bed. His entire body was in spasms and his face was contorted with pain. Yuko introduced us and found out the woman's name was Mayumi and her son was Kenji.

I watched as Yuko slowly brought Bailey to Kenji's bedside.

"*Hōmon* (Visit)," she said, as she placed a cloth on the edge of his bed and Bailey rested his chin on it. Mayumi smiled and lifted Kenji's clenched fist, placing it on Bailey's head. His face began to relax as she carefully stroked his hand across Bailey's ear.

I turned to Yuko.

"Will you ask if she would like Bailey to lie next to him on the bed?"

Mayumi nodded her head eagerly in reply.

"*Janpu* (Jump on)," said Yuko, followed by "*dakko* (snuggle)."

Bailey gently lay next to Kenji and rested his big white head across the boy's chest. Then an amazing thing happened. Kenji's whole body began to relax, and his expression became peaceful. I looked across at his mom, who was talking to Yuko. I noticed the tears falling behind her mask. They were looking at me as she spoke, and Yuko nodded.

"She asked me to tell you thank you for bringing Bailey here to the hospital. This is the first time her son has stopped having seizures in days."

I forced back tears as Mayumi picked up a picture frame from the bedside table and showed it to me. It had a photo of a smiling boy in a baseball uniform, holding a bat across his shoulder. She spoke to Yuko once more.

"She wants you to know that this is her son, Kenji. He was the star of his baseball team until a few weeks ago when he got sick."

I smiled at him and held Kenji's hand in mine.

"He is a very handsome boy," I said to his mom as Yuko translated. "I hope he feels better soon. We'll bring Bailey back to see him again."

As we said goodbye and left the room, I looked back at them and thought that if Kenji was the only person Bailey ever helped, it would have all been worth it.

Over the years, Bailey's popularity grew, and he became somewhat of a celebrity in Japan. He starred in a television show and was also featured in a worldwide documentary on the healing power of animals. He was even invited to attend an international summit between the United States and Japan and got to meet with both first ladies. Kim talked about the impact of the facility dog program and the successful collaboration between the two countries. Thankfully, Bailey didn't let the fame go to his head. He remained humble and committed to the children he visited every day.

When Bailey was ten years old, Shine On! Kids decided to have an early retirement party for him. Will and I were invited to attend, along with Bailey's puppy raisers, Sharon and Ron. We traveled to Japan and when we arrived at the children's hospital in Tokyo, where Bailey had worked for the past several years, we were amazed by the hundreds of people there to honor him. There were television crews, former patients and their families, and current patients, some of whom had been brought to the auditorium in their wheelchairs or hospital beds. Posters of Bailey with patients over the years lined the walls of the auditorium.

Many people spoke that afternoon about the impact Bailey had on their lives. One was a patient Bailey had visited very early in his career. She was now in nursing school, with plans to become a hospital dog handler when she graduated. Because of Bailey's success, many more hospital dogs began working at children's hospitals in Japan over the next several years.

The hospital director concluded the program with this: "Bailey's arrival was a groundbreaking, life-changing, and vision-changing event in Japan. He has helped thousands of children over the past nine years, and we are very grateful." I was so thankful for Kim's vision and Yuko's dedication that had made this partnership such a success.

As we were standing at the elevator on our way out, a middle-aged woman came hurrying toward us. She spoke excitedly to Kana but was looking directly at me.

"She is from Shizuoka," Kana translated. "She heard about Bailey's ceremony and came all the way here hoping to see you. She met you nine years ago when Bailey was just starting." The woman smiled and took a picture out of her purse and handed it to me. It was a picture of a boy in a baseball uniform. "Her name is Mayumi and her son's name is Kenji. Bailey visited her son for many years and helped him when nothing else could. She came here to tell you thank you."

14

Sam the Late Bloomer

Live your life and forget your age.
Norman Vincent Peale

I woke up with the sun and tiptoed into the living room. I peeked around the curtain and saw them all sleeping outside. Will had constructed a small fenced area on our lanai to corral the growing puppies. I couldn't believe they were already eight weeks old or that it was time for them to go to their new homes. Oliver caught me peeking and I waved to him. He smiled back at me and swished his tail. Surrounded by eleven sleeping puppies, Mr. Mom looked perfectly content.

Will and I loved all the puppies, but our personal favorite had always been the red-collared puppy named Sam. He was an exuberant pup with a fun-loving personality and always made us laugh. However, he was also quite stubborn and very independent! Not exactly the traits we were looking for in assistance dogs. Whenever someone arrived at the door, Sam felt compelled to greet them with something in his mouth. He usually ran into the bedroom and came out with a tennis shoe or a dirty sock from the laundry basket.

We wanted to keep Sam but felt it wouldn't be fair to him. We spent so much time with the dogs in the program that we were afraid we wouldn't have enough to spend with a dog of our own. Over the next week, all the puppies went to their new homes—except for Sam. But eventually we found a great home for him with a nice lady in Lahaina and had to say goodbye. We thought about him often and he was the only dog I ever regretted giving up.

Three years later, I was working at the campus when my cell phone rang. I pulled the phone out of my pocket, puzzled to see the caller was the Humane Society.

"Hello, Mo, this is Sandy, from the Humane Society. Do you have a moment to talk about one of our dogs?"

"Of course; how can I help?" I knew the Humane Society received thousands of dogs every year, but they had never called us about one before.

"We have a very nice golden retriever here," she said hopefully. "He's about three years old, and I think he might be a good dog for your program."

"Thank you so much for thinking of us, Sandy," I said, choosing my words carefully. "But we need to know the background of our dogs for health and temperament screening. We also start training them from the time they are puppies."

She sounded disappointed but thanked me and said they would try to find a good home for him.

A few days later, during a staff meeting, Cate mentioned that she had stopped by the Humane Society looking for candidates to send to the hearing dog school on the mainland.

"There's a beautiful golden retriever there," she said. "He looks just like one of our dogs."

"That must be the one they called me about," I said.

"His name is Sam," she added.

"That's funny, we had a golden named Sam too."

"The information sheet said he came from Lahaina."

"What a coincidence, our Sam lived in Lahaina too!"

Then it dawned on me—could this be our Sam? I raced to the phone and called the Humane Society and got a recording. I ran to the car and drove down the hill to the shelter. I still couldn't imagine how our Sam could be at the Humane Society. I prayed I wasn't too late.

I parked my car and ran through the lobby and back to the kennel area. I scanned the kennels for a golden retriever. My heart sank when I didn't see any. I was about to leave when I noticed that a middle-aged couple talking to one of the staff was blocking my view of a kennel. As I approached them, I saw a dog sitting in the very back of the kennel, holding a tattered stuffed animal and looking rather forlorn.

"Sam, is that you?" I asked.

His head flew up when he heard my voice, and he ran and jumped at the gate. *Yes, it's me!* he said with a smile and wagging tail. *Get me out of here!*

His paws touched my hands through the chain-link fence, and I reached in and scratched his neck. The kennel staff said, "I'm sorry, but this couple was here first and is considering adopting him."

My eyes filled with tears as I looked at them.

"Is this your dog?" the man asked.

"Well . . . not technically, but he was mine as a puppy."

There was an awkward pause.

"Please give us a minute," the woman said as they stepped away and spoke to each other.

When they returned, the woman smiled and said, "We'd like you to have him. We can see it's where he belongs."

As I completed the paperwork in the front office, I found out that his owner had passed away unexpectedly and a neighbor had brought him to the shelter.

Sam and I left the shelter together, and he happily jumped in the front seat of my car. He lay across my lap as we drove home, and I couldn't wait to surprise Will. We already had three black labs in training who were living with us at the time. When Will arrived home from work, he was enthusiastically greeted at the door by all the dogs. Sam jumped up and placed his paws on Will's chest and gently grabbed his arm in his mouth.

"Who's this one?" Will laughed.

"Guess!"

"He seems familiar, but I don't know . . ."

As if to help him out, Sam ran into our bedroom and came out with a tennis shoe in his mouth. He proudly presented it to Will, whose eyes widened in surprise.

"Is this Sammy?" he asked with a huge smile.

"Yes, it's him!" I explained what happened and we both were grateful that our beloved Sam had returned home to us. I reached out to Will, and Sam jumped up in between us for a group hug.

Sam was delighted to be on the campus and loved all the other dogs. He helped us raise dozens of puppies over the years and taught them many things, including the importance of respecting their elders. Whenever the puppies pounced on him and grabbed his ears or tail too hard, he showed them his "snaggle tooth." He curled his lip and gave the most vicious look he could manage, but they knew he was all bark and no bite.

Sam wanted desperately to join in whenever I was working with the other dogs in the training room. He sat in the courtyard and watched us closely through the glass doors. Once, when I had just finished a training session, Sam came running inside as I let the other dogs out. I'd been teaching them "tug," and Sam went right over to the door with the tug rope and pulled the door open, just like he'd watched the other dogs do! While he didn't get to work like the other dogs, Sam did have a job of sorts. He loved the camera and ended up being our program's model. Sam's smiling face graced our brochures and advertisements for many years. A picture of him holding a bunch of flowers was even on a bestselling greeting card!

Sam lived for our weekends at the beach. He somehow knew when it was Saturday and woke me up extra early by shoving a toy in my face with an excited expression, as if to say, *Let's go—time's a wastin'!* Sam loved every activity the beach had to offer, but his absolute favorite was digging for crabs. He looked for holes in the wet sand around the water's edge, where small sand crabs burrowed. Sam methodically sniffed each hole and knew which ones were occupied. He started digging and sometimes kept going until only the tip of his wagging tail was visible above the surface. He didn't catch one often, but occasionally we'd hear a yelp, and he'd resurface with a crab attached to his lip and frantically shake his head to dislodge it. Training assistance dogs is a serious business, and Sam provided comic relief both at home and on campus. He had a certain joie de vivre that lifted the spirits of everyone around him. It was impossible to be in a bad mood around Sam.

Sam was seven years old when I finished graduate school. Although my thesis was creating the sign language system, my studies were also focused on medical bio-detection. I was fascinated with the idea of dogs detecting cancer and other diseases, and I was fortunate to learn from some of the top researchers in this field.

A week after graduating in California, I was leading a team training camp back on Maui. There were three men in the class, all of whom had limited mobility and used wheelchairs. Sam sat alone in the courtyard and peered through the curtain into the training room, watching the dogs he had helped raise perform skills for their new partners.

During the first week of team training camp, two of the students developed urinary tract infections (UTIs) and one was hospitalized. This was the first time I realized how prevalent these infections are for many people with spinal cord injuries and other disabilities. Impaired bladder function and the use of catheters often contribute to this problem. To make matters worse, many people with neurological impairment don't have the typical warning signs—like pain. Left untreated, UTIs can quickly progress to kidney infections and life-threatening sepsis.

While visiting one student in the hospital, I began to wonder if dogs could be taught to detect UTIs, just like they could be taught to detect cancer. The idea intrigued me and the more I thought about it, the more excited I became about the potential this might have to provide early detection and perhaps even save lives. I was certain that with dogs' incredible sense of smell, they already knew when people had bacterial infections. They just needed to learn how to communicate that information.

I contacted one of my mentors from school, Dr. Michael McCulloch, who had conducted groundbreaking research on dogs detecting lung and breast cancer. He was intrigued by the idea and, much to my surprise, he immediately agreed to help me with the study. Dr. McCulloch helped to create the study design and protocol based on his earlier cancer detection studies. Kapiolani Medical Center and Clinical Laboratories agreed to partner with us on the project. The entire process was fascinating—I even liked the statistics and data processing. It took almost a year to finalize the protocol and receive the necessary approvals from the IRB (the hospital review board) and the IACUC (Institutional Animal Care and Use Committee) board that approves the use of animals in research studies.

The next step was to select the five dogs who would participate in the study. The criteria included that they had to be one to five years old and have high drive. We needed a minimum of ten dogs from which to choose. The problem was there were only nine dogs living on the campus at the time. Where were we going to find the tenth dog? I was pondering this as I gazed out the window and saw Sam smiling back at me from the courtyard. Could Sam try out for the study? He was well over the age limit at eight years old, and his white muzzle would certainly give him away. However, the tryouts were the next day, so I decided to give him a chance.

The dogs were brought into the training room one at a time. They were presented with the task of finding a dog treat hidden in one of several boxes placed on the floor. Sam was the last one to try out, and he approached the boxes with the same enthusiasm he had for everything in life. His tail wagged furiously as he searched the boxes and quickly found the hidden treat. At the end of the day, notes and score sheets were tallied by the evaluator, and the dogs who made the team were announced. The top performers were Scout, Sadie, Abe, Astro . . . and Sam! He finally had a job, and I couldn't have been prouder if he were my own son.

We cleared out the main training room, and the office adjacent to it was transformed into a laboratory. There were five stations where 12″ x 12″ scent-detection boxes were placed along the wall exactly twenty-six inches apart. The boxes were made of white Plexiglas and had a small circular opening at the top, which allowed the dogs to smell the contents but not reach inside. Each box contained a plastic tray that held a small glass vial containing a one-milliliter sample.

The laboratory on Oahu sent us about forty urine samples per day, each labeled with gender, age, whether it had tested positive or negative for bacteria, and what type of bacteria it contained. We picked them up at the airport in biohazard bags, and our staff wore protective equipment when unpacking and handling the samples.

The five dogs quickly learned to locate the boxes containing the target samples that tested positive for bacteria. The dogs took turns approaching the lineup and sniffed each box one at a time. We initially paired the target samples with a piece of dog kibble in the box. When they found the box with the target sample and kibble, we clicked and treated. They quickly associated the reward with the target scent and were soon able to locate the target without the kibble. They learned to ignore the many background odors in the negative samples and focus only on the samples containing bacteria.

In the beginning, each dog had their own natural alerting behavior when they found the target scent. Astro stopped and calmly stared at the correct box. Abe stood over the correct box and placed his nose in the hole while glancing back at me out of the corner of his eye. Sadie lay down next to the box and stared at it intently, and Scout spun around in a circle and then sat on the box with a triumphant smile.

Sam's natural alerting behavior was unique and came from years of doing his own scent detection work at the beach. When he approached the box containing the target scent, he started sniffing with the utmost concentration and wagged his tail in excitement. Then he began digging frantically at the small hole on top of the box! It was a clear signal but unfortunately resulted in boxes getting tipped over and knocked across the room. The next step was to teach all of the dogs the same "trained alert," which was to sit directly in front of the box containing the target scent.

A dog's sense of smell is more than one hundred thousand times stronger than a human's. The hardest part of the process was finding a way to sanitize the boxes that had contained the target scent well enough so the dogs wouldn't alert to the residual smell in those boxes on subsequent days. We eventually created a successful cleaning protocol, and the training phase progressed smoothly after that.

During the double-blind testing phase, neither the handlers nor the dogs knew what types of samples the boxes contained. We simply let each dog off leash and instructed them to "go find." We completed thousands of runs and I never grew tired of it, nor did the dogs. It was awe-inspiring to see them using their unique gift—their incredible sense of smell. They were all eager to work, but no one enjoyed it more than Sam. He had always been a free spirit, and I could tell he appreciated being able to work independently. He could hardly wait for his turn each day and approached every session with enthusiasm. Sam looked so proud to finally have a job!

We started with samples containing E. coli bacteria because it is the most common cause of UTIs. We began with full-strength samples and then diluted both the positive and negative samples to 1 percent urine in distilled water, and the dogs still had the same accuracy rate. Then we decided to try diluting the samples to 0.1 percent. We used a random number table for the order of the dogs, and Sam was first up! I watched from across the room and held my breath as he approached the lineup and began sniffing the boxes. Without

Courtesy of Ron Dahlquist, Dahlquist Photography

Medical Scent Detection Dog Sam

hesitation, he sat in front of the fourth box. I heard the click from inside the laboratory room, indicating he was correct.

"Good boy, Sammy. You did it!" I praised. He wagged his tail and looked very pleased with himself.

Proving the dogs could alert at low levels was important because it suggested that dogs might be able to identify early stages of infections, before they became life-threatening. The final stage of the study was teaching the dogs to alert to other types of bacteria that cause UTIs, including Staphylococcus, Enterococcus, and Klebsiella.

When the double-blind testing phase was completed, the statistician calculated the results. All the dogs had more than a 95 percent sensitivity rate (correctly alerting to a positive sample) and more than a 90 percent specificity rate (correctly ignoring a negative sample). Sam had the highest success rate of all. Later that year, the study was published in *Oxford Journals* and won their Editor's Choice Award. It was also mentioned in the *New England Journal of Medicine* and *National Geographic*. The following year, I was invited to present our research at the Inaugural International Conference on Medical Bio-Detection at Cambridge University in England. Who would have thought that our free spirited, sand crab–loving, beach bum, Sam, would find his calling so late in life and leave such a lasting legacy?

15

Super Trooper

A hero is an ordinary individual who finds the strength to persevere and endure in spite of overwhelming obstacles.

Christopher Reeve

Even as a puppy, Trooper seemed to be an old soul. He had a wise expression and was always calm and self-possessed. Unlike most puppies, he heeled perfectly on the leash and was not easily distracted. Sharon and her family began puppy raising Trooper soon after Bailey graduated. We received glowing monthly reports as he grew up.

When Trooper was twelve months old, he arrived on campus to begin advanced training. He was an honest dog, and I was impressed with his steadiness and strong work ethic. Trooper was born at the guide dog school in Australia and came from over fifty generations of the best guide dog lines in the world. Perhaps this was why he had such a dignified air about him. He was a handsome dog with a broad head and dark brown eyes that shone with kindness and intelligence. Trooper had the ideal temperament for a service dog and developed exceptionally strong skills. Although he wouldn't be ready to graduate for a few months, I checked our waiting list one day. I pictured him going to someone very special and prayed for Trooper to find his calling. I trusted the right person would come along at the right time.

A week later, I received an email from a young woman named Summer who was interested in applying for a service dog. Summer learned about ADH after Dr. Wendi and Hospital Dog Tucker from Kapiolani Medical Center had given a presentation at Iolani High School, and Summer was contacted by her former teacher. As soon as I read her email, I had a feeling that Trooper might be the perfect dog for her.

We spoke on the phone, and Summer shared a little bit about her life and why she wanted a service dog. Summer was a bright and personable young woman who had grown up on Oahu, where she enjoyed kayaking and paddling. She was an excellent student and attended Pacific University before moving to Boston for the MBA program at Northeastern University. She worked overseas for a couple of years before moving back home to Hawaii. She was twenty-six years old when she returned to the islands, and her future could not have been any brighter. She had no idea that her life was about to change forever. One day, Summer began to feel sick and developed a fever. Her condition quickly worsened and her parents drove her to the ER. She was soon diagnosed with bacterial meningitis. In order to save her life, the doctors made the difficult decision to amputate all four of her limbs.

Summer spent over a year at the Queen's Medical Center before being transferred to an inpatient rehabilitation center in Portland, Oregon. She lived there for two years, while she underwent several more surgeries and learned how to use her prostheses. She also learned how to navigate life without the use of her limbs. Most of the other residents at the rehab center were her grandparents' age and Summer became good friends with many of them. I was impressed with her positive attitude, although she admitted she sometimes felt lonely.

During the interview, Summer let me know that she wanted a dog to help her with tasks around the house and also out in public. She shared that she felt nervous about coming back to Hawaii and seeing people for the first time without her limbs. She hoped that having a service dog by her side would help take some attention off of her. As we talked, I felt honored to have the chance to help this courageous young woman who had already overcome so much.

Summer was over the moon with excitement when she found out that her service dog application had been approved and she was matched with Trooper. It seemed like perfect timing because the next team training camp coincided with her long-awaited return home to Hawaii. She couldn't wait to come to Maui and meet her new partner. However, a week before her departure, Summer found out that she had to have yet another surgery and that it would delay her travel plans by a couple of months. She was so disappointed to miss the team training and was discouraged that she would be celebrating her thirtieth birthday alone and so far from home. I assured her that we would continue training Trooper, and he would wait for her as long as it took.

I enjoyed working with Trooper and teaching him specialized skills to help Summer. She was determined to become as independent as possible and had a long list of things she wanted Trooper to assist her with. He learned how to open the dishwasher and pull out the racks, get a drink out of the refrigerator, and bring Summer her cell phone. He also learned how to place laundry into the washing machine and take it out of the dryer. He didn't actually fold the clothes, but his always earnest expression gave the impression he would have if he could. Trooper learned to open the kitchen cabinet and drop items into the trash bin. To make sure Summer had room to maneuver in her wheelchair, he also learned to pick up his toys off the floor and put them away in a basket.

While waiting for Summer to return from the mainland, I visited her family's home in Honolulu to learn more about where she and Trooper would be living. Her mother showed me around their beautiful home, and I got to meet the rest of her family. I was touched to see how much love would surround Summer when she was finally allowed to return home. I stood in her bedroom and thought about all the life Summer still had to live and how Trooper could help her experience it fully. I wondered what else I could teach him.

Before I left, I had an idea.

"May I borrow one of Summer's spare prosthetics?" I asked her mother.

She looked at me, puzzled.

"I want to use it to train Trooper," I explained. "Using a prosthetic arm will help him learn how to retrieve objects and give them to Summer."

She agreed and loaned me a prosthetic arm that had two metal hooks that pinched together to pick things up.

I returned to our campus and went right to work. I taught Trooper to bring me the prosthetic arm and then had him deliver items to me while I used it. I had to be careful not to pinch his lips or whiskers when grabbing things out of his mouth with the hooks. Trooper was incredibly patient and trusting. The more I worked with Trooper, the more I had a sense that he was going to dramatically change Summer's life.

Two weeks before she was due home, Summer called to let me know there was going to be another delay in her homecoming while she waited for the fitting of her new prostheses. She was so disappointed and worried that she would lose out on Trooper, whose picture she kept on her nightstand. I had taught Trooper every skill I could think of, and he was more than ready to graduate. It wasn't fair to him to wait any longer. Will and I talked it over that night, and he suggested, "Why don't we take Trooper to Portland and do the training with her there?" The next day I called Summer, and she was thrilled with the idea. We made plane reservations and booked a hotel for two weeks near the rehab facility.

Will, Trooper, and I settled into our bulkhead seats for the flight to Portland. It was just under six hours, and Trooper lay at our feet the entire flight. It was Trooper's first time traveling in the cabin, but he took it all in stride. I petted him and gave him treats during the takeoff and landing to help make it a positive experience. He was so quiet and well behaved, the other passengers didn't even know he was there.

When we reached cruising altitude, I tucked my feet under me, settling in between Will and the window. I'd brought a book to read but was distracted by thoughts of Summer. I reflected on all she had been through and prayed that she and Trooper would have a long and happy life together.

Summer and Service Dog Trooper

When we landed in Portland, Will went to pick up the rental car while Trooper and I waited for the luggage. An hour later, we arrived at the hotel, and the three of us checked in and took a walk along the Willamette River. Much to everyone's delight, Trooper practiced carrying a shopping bag in his mouth and pushed the automatic button to open the door to the hotel. It was a lovely evening, but we headed to bed early so we could be prepared for the next day.

We arrived at the rehabilitation center at eight a.m. and went straight to Summer's room. Trooper heeled by Will's side as we wove our way past nurses doing their morning rounds and staff pushing noisy carts of breakfast trays. I tried unsuccessfully to contain my excitement as we kept an eye out for Summer's room.

Finally, we turned a corner and saw her room number. The door was partially open, and there was a cheerful, handwritten yellow sign taped to it that read, "Welcome Trooper!" I smiled and rubbed Trooper's ear. He looked even more dapper than usual with his brand-new blue graduate coat and collar. Will knocked lightly and we entered the room.

The morning light streamed through the only window, illuminating a pretty young woman with long black hair, sitting on the bed. She wasn't wearing her prosthetics, and I caught my breath when I saw her exposed limbs and the scars of all her surgeries.

A smile lit up her entire face as she greeted us. "Trooper, you're here!" she exclaimed in delight and called him up onto the bed. The normally stoic Trooper didn't need to be asked twice and jumped right up on the bed. He sat next to Summer and gave her a quick kiss on the cheek. If he was surprised by her appearance, he never showed it. Dogs have a wonderful way of looking right past our outward appearance and directly into our souls.

"Hi, Summer!" Will said as he gave her a hug. "We're so happy to finally meet you."

Once I met Summer, any concerns I had melted away. She was so positive that it was easy to focus on the journey ahead rather than all the suffering she had been through in the past.

I admired her confidence and how comfortable she was in her own skin. So many of us get bogged down with how we look and worry about what other people think. Summer had a quick wit and great sense of humor, and it was impossible to feel sad around her.

I noticed there was a dog bed covered with toys in the corner of her room, along with a bowl of water on the floor. She showed us a cabinet that had drawers stocked with Trooper's grooming supplies, along with leashes, collars, dog biscuits, jerky treats, tennis balls, KONGs, a Frisbee, and a wide variety of stuffed animals. Trooper had clearly arrived in the land of plenty!

We trained each day in the rehab facility and surrounding neighborhood. Summer was thrilled that Trooper knew how to pick up all kinds of items and carefully present them to her so she could grasp them with her prosthetic hand. She appreciated that Trooper could push the door button so she could exit the facility without having to ask anyone for help. We practiced the list of the ninety cues that Trooper knew. The two of them continued to amaze me every step of the way.

Summer enjoyed being outside, and we took long walks each afternoon. There were lots of barking dogs nearby, and Summer was relieved that Trooper completely ignored them. One afternoon, we had just returned from a walk, and I trailed behind the pair down the hallway. I was admiring how beautifully Trooper was heeling next to Summer as they made their way back to her room. Suddenly, a man walking on high stilts came around the corner toward them on his way to change a light bulb. At the same time, a dog ran out of one of the rooms, barking ferociously at the man and then turned his attention to Trooper. I held my breath, knowing I was too far away to help. The stilts alone were distracting enough, but an aggressive dog could be a disaster. Summer stayed calm and confident as she talked to Trooper and kept going past all the commotion. Trooper didn't bat an eye. I knew in that moment they were going to be an incredible team.

Summer had such a positive attitude and was determined to become independent. Each morning, she methodically went through the slow and painstaking process of putting on each prosthesis. I never once heard her complain about anything. Spending time with Summer helped me to put into perspective the things that I might be tempted to complain about. With patience, she became skilled at grooming and feeding Trooper on her own. She was very affectionate with him, and after two weeks of training, their bond was solid and their teamwork was excellent. It was time for us to leave Trooper with Summer and fly home to Maui.

A month later, Summer was finally allowed to return home with Trooper by her side. I spent another week training with them on Oahu at her home and all the places she frequented. Summer was eager to return to her job as an accountant in downtown Honolulu, but in order to do so, she needed to drive. While Summer learned to drive a car using her prosthetic limbs, Trooper learned to ride "shotgun" with his seat belt on.

"Trooper's the perfect dog for me," she told me over lunch one day. "He is always such a gentleman."

"What do you mean?" I asked.

"Well, for one thing, he knows I don't like slobbery kisses or getting dog hair on my bed. So, he's learned to give me a kiss by barely touching my cheek. He also knows to sleep on his blanket at the foot of my bed."

At the mention of his name, Trooper glanced up at Summer and wagged his tail expectantly.

"And look at that tail," she laughed. "I love it. He's always ready to help. Sometimes I think of extra things for him to do, just because he likes helping me so much."

A month after returning home, Summer invited me to attend a speech she was giving at her former high school about the importance of gratitude. Like me, she had always been afraid of public speaking, but she had gained a newfound confidence and courage during her time in the hospital. More than anything, she wanted to share with the students what she'd learned about perseverance and the importance of having a positive attitude.

The auditorium was packed as Summer slowly wheeled past the bleachers and onto the stage with Trooper by her side. Her smiling face peeked out above the colorful flower lei the staff and students had given her in honor of the occasion. She smiled down at Trooper, and he gazed up at her adoringly. She took a deep breath as she looked out at the crowd and began to speak. She concluded by saying that although she would never feel a wedding ring on her finger or her toes in the sand, she had someone who loved her unconditionally, and that was enough. When she finished, there was not a dry eye in the room. Everyone in the auditorium was so moved by her message they gave her a long standing ovation.

Trooper was Summer's constant companion over the years and was a great icebreaker for her out in public. Instead of seeing a woman with a disability, people saw a beautiful team that was living life to the fullest. With Trooper by her side, Summer enjoyed greater independence and traveled everywhere. According to Summer, Trooper's favorite places to visit were the wineries in Oregon and Napa Valley. She said that although he preferred country life, he also tolerated their trips to Las Vegas like a champ.

Over the years, Summer's confidence increased, and she and Trooper went on many adventures together. They traveled all the way to Washington, DC, together where Summer received an award from the Pentagon for the most outstanding government employee with a disability.

One day, Will and I were on Oahu picking up two new puppies, Mac and Noah. After taking them to visit the children's hospital, we stopped by to check in on Summer and Trooper. It was great to see how happy they were together. She tossed a ball in the pool for Trooper, who leaped into the water to retrieve it. We all watched while Trooper tried to give Mac and Noah swimming lessons. Mac jumped right into the pool after him, while Noah decided to sit on the step and observe. Afterward, they all tumbled around on the grass and played "bite the face" until they finally flopped down under the shade of a palm tree and fell fast asleep.

"You know," said Summer thoughtfully as she looked at the sleeping dogs. "If I had just one wish, it wouldn't be to have my arms and legs back."

"Really?" I asked with surprise. "What would you wish for?"

"All I really want is for Trooper to know how much I love and appreciate him," she said. "He is so brave. Even when he is afraid of trying something new, he always does his best and never gives up. He is my hero." My heart swelled at hearing her words. They really were two of a kind.

16

Tucker Fulfills His Purpose

The best way to find yourself is to lose yourself in the service of others.

Mahatma Gandhi

Blissfully unaware that our conversation would determine his fate, Tucker lay stretched out on his back on the dog bed on the office floor. His golden tail swished back and forth as he looked up at me with a silly grin. I slipped off my shoe under the table and rubbed his chest with my bare foot.

His coat was a gleaming gold and had somehow maintained the silky softness it had as a puppy. Even at a year old, Tucker was often mistaken for a puppy. He had a huge round head and big paws, which made him look like he still had some growing to do. His ears were thick and soft and lay flat against his head. His expression was kind, and he had a constant twinkle in his eye.

I thought about the first time Will and I visited the hospital with him on Christmas Day. After seeing the miraculous impact that he had on Lili, I knew he was destined to become a hospital dog. The application from Kapiolani Medical Center had arrived when Tucker was in advanced training, and he was now ready to graduate. The children's hospital was the perfect placement for him. I remembered my own childhood stays in the hospital and was so excited about all the keiki he would be able to help.

"We have three more people who are interested in being his handler," the hospital administrator was saying. "But I don't think any of these will be the right fit either. One works in accounting, one works only part-time, and the other already has five dogs at home."

My heart sank as I listened. We'd been having a surprisingly difficult time finding a handler for Tucker over the past several months. Someone even recommended that I should give up, which of course only prompted me to try harder. They thought the challenges I'd encountered suggested it wasn't meant to be. However, knowing from experience that the biggest obstacles often appear right before the biggest blessings, I was determined to press on. Deep in my heart, I believed Tucker was destined to have a profound impact on many children, and I refused to get discouraged. Patience and perseverance!

"There was one person who would have been perfect for the job, but unfortunately she lives in a condo that doesn't allow dogs," she continued as she looked through the applications.

"Can you tell me more about her?" I asked, intrigued.

"Her name is Wendi Hirsch, and she is a child psychologist. She's been here for about seven years and is married to her job. She is wonderful with the patients, and the staff love her too."

"Perhaps I could meet her and see if there might be a way to work things out?" I asked hopefully.

Ten minutes later, Wendi had joined us in the office and was sitting on the floor petting Tucker. She was so friendly and funny that I liked her immediately. It looked like it was love at first sight for Tucker too, who was getting a belly rub.

The next day Wendi called to let me know that the condo manager had denied her request, so she had decided to move. I was impressed by her commitment, and a month later I was conducting the home interview at her new, dog-friendly condo.

That spring, Wendi came to Maui for team training camp. When the first quiz was handed out, she shared with the class how nervous she was and how afraid she was of not passing the tests.

"Come on, you're a doctor." I laughed. "I'm pretty sure you've got this."

She still sounded doubtful, so I added, "We've had a ten-year-old who passed the test," hoping this would ease her mind.

"Stop—you're making it worse!" She moaned as the class laughed.

I was determined to relieve her anxiety, so I continued. "Trust me; you'll do fine. No one has ever failed the class before."

"So . . . I would be the first?" she asked with a look of horror as I handed out the quizzes.

Wendi passed the first quiz and began to relax as the week went on. She'd never had a dog before, so she was starting with the basics. Before the first practice session, we handed out leashes to the students. Wendi looked at the leash for a minute and studied both ends. I watched as she clipped the buckle to her belt loop and then took the handle of the leash and tried to slide it over Tucker's head.

"I'm going to need a bigger leash; this one doesn't fit him," she announced. I tried my best to keep a straight face as I explained that the buckle end attached to his collar, and the loop end of the leash went in her hand. Tucker was very patient and tried to help her as much as he could.

We use an "eh" or "ch" sound to instruct the dogs to stop a certain behavior. It needs to be said in a firm tone for the dog to understand. When dogs communicate vocally with each other, they use low tones to send away and high tones to call toward them.

"Okay, class, repeat after me." I said "eh" in my firmest voice.

"Eh," the students replied in unison. All had an appropriate low tone except for Wendi, whose "eh" sounded downright cheerful. An otherwise excellent student, this was her biggest struggle. Not just during the class, but throughout Tucker's career, she never could sound stern with him. Fortunately, he never gave her reason to.

A month later, I visited them at the hospital for a follow-up visit, and what I witnessed was pure magic. A nurse had paged Wendi for a "Tucker consult" in the cancer unit, where a patient was refusing to take their medicine. She and Tucker responded immediately, with me trailing close behind.

I could hear a child sobbing from halfway down the hall. When we entered the room, a darling four-year-old boy sat on the hospital bed, hugging his knees to his chest. His face was red, and his eyes were swollen from crying. As soon as he saw Tucker, he grew quiet.

Dr. Wendi introduced herself and said, "Look, Tucker is going to take his medicine."

"See?" she said with a bright smile, holding out her hand so the little boy could see the golden capsule. It contained fish oil, which was good for Tucker's heart and coat. "Would you like to watch him take his medicine?" He nodded eagerly.

Tucker watched intently as the boy wiped the tears from his face. Tucker knew the routine. Wendi asked him to sit and then gave him the capsule. He swallowed it in one gulp. Then, for the grand finale, he gave a loud burp and wagged his tail. The boy giggled.

"Okay, now it's your turn," Dr. Wendi said. The nurse handed the boy his pill with a paper cup of water, and he swallowed it. Then he looked over at Tucker with a big smile and gave a pretend burp.

Wendi's job at the children's hospital included counseling sessions and making rounds to visit patients in their rooms, on the oncology unit, and in the playroom. She was also the one who had to meet with parents and give them the devastating news when their child had a serious diagnosis.

Tucker accompanied Wendi everywhere throughout the hospital. He was incredibly intuitive with the patients and always seemed to know what each child needed at any given moment. He provided courage to children as he escorted them to surgery and was there to comfort them when they got out. He provided a distraction for children while their port was installed and snuggled with them while they received chemotherapy. Tucker also helped provide motivation for patients each day during their physical therapy sessions. Children often made an extra effort to walk toward Tucker or reach for him, knowing the reward was getting to hug him and feel his soft fur. Tucker had a special presence and intention in his interactions that made everyone feel like they were his personal favorite.

Tucker had funny habits the children loved. One was lying spread-eagle on the cool hospital floor in his impersonation of a bear rug. The thing that delighted children to no end was when Tucker burped. They always laughed hysterically, and since there was no medical reason found for his burping, I honestly think that's why he did it. Tucker loved to make people happy and would do anything for a laugh.

The medical staff appreciated Tucker's presence, and Wendi often received pages from nurses and doctors for a "Tucker consult." When children were afraid of getting an IV installed, Tucker would arrive on the scene, and the mood would instantly change. Many children were so terrified of getting IVs that it was challenging for the nurses to install them. Tucker provided a great distraction. While children petted and talked to Tucker, their veins relaxed, and the IVs slipped in unnoticed.

Tucker was unflappable in all situations. He was incredibly confident and self-contained. Once, I was visiting the hospital on Halloween and was feeling a bit underdressed with all the great costumes everyone was wearing. I was making rounds with Tucker (who was dressed as a hot dog) and Wendi (who was a bottle of ketchup). The elevator doors opened, and we were suddenly face-to-face with Chewbacca from Star Wars (the hospital chaplain), who was seven feet tall. I jumped about a foot off the floor. When I landed, I looked over at Tucker to see what his reaction was. As usual, he was much more composed than I was and merely wagged his tail in a friendly greeting to Chewbacca. Although most dogs don't enjoy getting dressed up, Tucker seemed to recognize the humor in it and appreciated all the laughter and extra attention.

Wendi served on several boards and participated in various meetings throughout the week. One was the hospital board meeting, which took place every Monday morning at seven a.m. There were usually about twenty physicians in attendance. The first time she brought Tucker, he calmly acknowledged the others in the room. Wendi took a place at the long, koa wood table, and Tucker, noticing an empty seat beside her, slowly stepped up onto the chair, sat down, and gazed solemnly at the doctors gathered around the table. They all burst out laughing and from then on, a seat at the table was always reserved for Tucker. Sometimes, when things got tense, Tucker would let out a burp to help lighten the mood.

Tucker soon became the face of the hospital. He had thousands of followers on social media and helped with the fundraising campaign for the new wing of the hospital. When the old garage was demolished, Tucker pushed a button with his paw to ignite the explosion. When the groundbreaking ceremony took place, Tucker was on the front page of the newspaper, wearing a hard hat and orange vest, digging a hole in the ground. When there was an opening ceremony for the new wing, there was Tucker, riding in the passenger seat of a convertible driven by the CEO. Tucker rested his elbow on the armrest and smiled benevolently upon the cheering crowd that had gathered for the ceremony. I laughed when I saw him on the news, because I could tell that he thought everyone was there to see him, and perhaps they were.

The hospital held a "prom" each spring for the patients, who all dressed up in formal attire. Tucker attended each year in a tuxedo and posed for pictures with the keiki as their prom date. Many children stayed in touch with him years after being discharged. Tucker was often their most lasting memory of their time at the hospital.

Many patients returned to the hospital for ongoing treatment. For the first time, parents reported that their children were looking forward to coming back because they would get to see Tucker. Other children, like Kendon, rarely left the hospital and looked forward to seeing Tucker every day. Kendon was one of Tucker's favorite people. They'd known each other since Kendon was a baby. Tucker loved the way Kendon gently petted the crimped hair on his ears and the sweet sound of his giggle.

Kendon's family was from the Big Island, and they all loved Tucker as much as he did. When Kendon was two years old, they started the Tucker Fan Club, and Kendon was appointed the first president. Kendon learned to talk while he was in the hospital, and the first word he said was "Tucker." Tucker was usually very stingy with his kisses, even when people asked for one. With Kendon, he couldn't resist sneaking a quick kiss on his cheek or arm. Each time he did this, Kendon giggled uncontrollably and said, "Tucker tickles!" Kendon's family loved seeing him laugh and were thankful for the big golden teddy bear who made him so happy.

Kendon often fell asleep while hugging Tucker. Tucker lay with his head across the little boy's chest and felt his heart beating. The nurses noticed that Kendon's heart rate and blood pressure lowered whenever he was with Tucker.

One day, as they snuggled together, Tucker's nose twitched as he smelled something different on Kendon's breath.

Tucker knew. He had noticed that same acrid odor on many of the cancer patients before. He knew that sometimes the smell went away, and the child got stronger and everyone was happy. He also knew that sometimes the smell got stronger and the child went away, and everyone was sad.

The following Monday, Tucker paused at the doorway as he and Dr. Wendi were entering Kendon's room. Surprised by his hesitation, Dr. Wendi looked down at him and noticed that his nose was twitching.

He sniffed several times just to be sure. The smell was getting stronger. He looked at Kendon sleeping on the bed and noticed he was very pale.

"Tucker, let's go," Wendi said, encouraging him to enter the room. She placed a sheet across the bed and said, "Tucker, jump on." Before she could say "snuggle," Tucker curled up next to Kendon and gave him a gentle kiss on the cheek. Kendon's eyes fluttered open and he gave a small smile.

"Tucker tickles," he whispered. They spent extra time with Kendon that day, as he drifted in and out of consciousness. It was eventually time to go, since they had an appointment with another patient.

"Goodbye, Kendon. We'll see you tomorrow," Dr. Wendi said. "Tucker, let's go." He laid his head across Kendon's chest and refused to move. "Let's go," she repeated, and again he wouldn't budge.

She had only seen Tucker disobey like this a few times before. Each time, it had been with patients who were near the end of their lives. She wasn't sure how, but Tucker seemed to know when a child's time was getting close and didn't want to leave their side. Her eyes filled with tears as she held his collar and lured him off the bed with a treat. Tucker stopped at the doorway to look back at his friend and hung his head as they walked away. Kendon went to heaven that afternoon.

Later that year, Wendi and I were invited to speak at an assistance dog conference in Buenos Aires, Argentina. We gave a presentation about hospital dogs, which were a new concept in that region. Medical professionals and dog trainers from across South America attended and learned about the physical, psychological, emotional, and social benefits that hospital dogs provide. Wendi shared stories and pictures of Tucker. She talked about Tucker's friendship with Kendon and what a huge blessing he had been during Kendon's short life.

Wendi and Hospital Dog Tucker

Afterward, we provided informational handouts to several attendees who were interested in starting hospital dog programs in their countries.

We returned to Hawaii, and Wendi went back to work with Tucker. As a psychologist, she understood the needs of her patients. She also made sure to take care of Tucker's needs. She took him on walks twice a day and had regularly scheduled playtimes and nap times for him. He still loved to play with coconuts, and Wendi made sure he always had one nearby.

Each weekend, they went on a long walk through Kapiolani Park in Waikiki. Tucker was a bit of a snob with other dogs and usually ignored their attempts to interact with him. He'd simply raise his nose and turn his head away, sending a clear message that he would not dignify their attempts to play with a response.

One day they were taking a new route through the middle of the park when Tucker suddenly started pulling on the leash. Wendi was surprised since he usually walked so calmly beside her. But today he was forging ahead, wagging his tail, and pulling her across the grass, away from the path. She looked around to see what he was so excited about and saw a yellow lab chasing a Frisbee. The dog was proudly returning it to her owner as Tucker ran up to them in greeting.

"I'm so sorry," Wendi said breathlessly as she looked up at the dog's owner. She couldn't help but notice how handsome he was when he smiled and said, "That's okay, but Sadie doesn't really like to play with other dogs. She only has eyes for the Frisbee."

Tucker was doing a play bow, with his chest toward the ground, his hindquarters in the air, and his tail wagging quickly. Sadie did a play bow and went nose-to-nose with him, then suddenly spun around and ran across the lawn. Tucker chased after her as the leash slipped through Wendi's fingers.

"She—" "He—"

"—never does this," they finished in unison and laughed.

"My name's Barry, and that's Sadie. She's ten years old."

"So is Tucker," she said. "My name's Wendi." They chatted easily while the dogs chased each other across the lawn and rolled happily on the freshly cut grass.

When the dogs finally tired themselves out, Barry said, "We're down here most Saturdays around this time if you'd like to let them play again."

"That would be great," Wendi replied. "We'll see you next weekend."

"Good boy, Tucker," she whispered as they walked away and she glanced back at Barry, who smiled and waved. The play-dates for the dogs soon turned into real dates for the humans. Barry and Wendi's relationship grew as Tucker and Sadie enjoyed a golden year's romance of their own.

One morning my phone rang, and I saw it was Wendi. I was looking forward to her usual cheerful greeting but instead, her voice was quivering.

"I think there's something wrong with Tucker."

"What is it?" I asked, my heart filling with dread.

"He seems kind of lethargic, and he's put on two pounds."

I breathed a sigh of relief, grateful for such minor symptoms.

"Well, he is getting older, so it might just be that his metabolism is slowing down."

"His stomach also looks bigger. Something just doesn't seem right."

"Maybe you should take him to the vet and get him checked out." It would have been easy to dismiss her concerns, but I knew how close they were and trusted her instincts.

Wendi had Tucker rest in her office the remainder of the morning and drove him to the vet after lunch. She glanced over at Tucker, who was sitting in the passenger seat with his elbow leaning on the armrest as he looked out the window. She saw his nose twitching and thought he was smelling the ocean across the street.

Tucker twitched his nose and smelled it again. It was even stronger than the smell of the ocean. He tilted his head and tried to detect which direction it was coming from. It was the same acrid smell that some of the patients had. It had been following him everywhere for weeks and was steadily getting stronger.

That afternoon, Tucker was diagnosed with cancer.

A month later, the sun was low on the horizon, and the air was beginning to cool as a long line of people entered Central Union Church to pay their respects. The wooden shutters lay back against the thick stone walls as the afternoon trade winds blew in through the tall arched windows. The church was established in 1833 and had held memorial services for many of Hawaii's dignitaries.

Hawaiian ladies wearing muumuus handed out a lei and a program to each of the guests as they entered and made their way to the wooden pews. The sweet scent of plumeria flowers filled the large room. Orange rays from the evening sun shone through the window and cast a heavenly glow on the picture of Tucker that stood on the altar next to the pulpit. It was as if all of nature wanted to join in this celebration of his life and pay their respects. The aloha spirit was palpable as I watched everyone greeting and hugging each other.

From my seat up on the stage, behind the pulpit, I watched in awe as the church filled up. I had never been on this side of the pulpit before, and the perspective was quite different. Will was smiling at me from the front row. Sitting next to him was Tucker's puppy raiser, Elaine, whose current puppy-in-training, Cassie, was lying at her feet. Across from them were Lili and her mom, whom Tucker had met as a puppy on Christmas Day. There were hundreds of guests and dozens of volunteers. I recognized several patients and many of the hospital staff, whom I had gotten to know over the years. Most of the people I didn't recognize, but my heart swelled as I realized that Tucker knew all of them and had been a blessing to each one. I was filled with the most profound feeling of joy and sensed that God was right there among us and smiling too. I sat between the hospital chaplain and Wendi, whose hand was holding tightly on to mine, as the church pastor stood up to welcome the guests and begin the ceremony.

Several patients and family members shared the impact Tucker had on their lives, including Kendon's grandmother, who had flown in from the Big Island. Lili and her mom talked about Tucker's part in her miraculous recovery. The hospital chaplain shared how Tucker had assisted him in ministering to so many families. Next it was Wendi's turn to talk, and I gave her hand a squeeze as she approached the podium. She described how Tucker had been a blessing not just for the patients but he had been the biggest blessing in her life too.

As I listened to her talk, a feeling of overwhelming gratitude welled up inside of me. Time stood still as I pictured the moment I first met Tucker at the airport and the Christmas morning when we discovered his calling in life. I thought about how he had the gift of making everyone feel special. I was so thankful for Tucker and Wendi and all the thousands of lives they had touched. I was grateful for all the people who helped make this possible, like Elaine and Tucker's sponsor, Mary. I felt eternally thankful that Tucker had found his purpose in life. In doing so, he had helped me to fulfill my purpose also.

I heard the applause as Wendi finished her speech and the chaplain said, "Our last speaker is Mo Maurer, founder of Assistance Dogs of Hawaii. She is Tucker's trainer and the person responsible for bringing him to the hospital."

I approached the pulpit and looked out at all the faces in the packed church. For once, I felt completely calm and at peace as I began to speak to the crowd.

"Ten years ago, my husband, Will, and I brought Tucker to visit the hospital for the first time. It was on Christmas Day. He was just a puppy and looked like a big teddy bear. I knew right away that he was destined to work with children." I took a deep breath and fought back tears as I continued. "Tucker has a special place in my heart because I spent so much of my own childhood in the hospital. My earliest memories are from there. I can relate to what many of you have gone through and am so thankful for the blessing Tucker has been to so many children and their families."

Rule #10: ~~Don't ever cry in front of clients.~~

It was a beautiful celebration, and even though we were all heavyhearted that Tucker was no longer with us, no one could deny the profound impact he had on each one of us.

We returned to Maui, and Will built a beautiful wheelchair-accessible tree house on our campus in memory of Tucker.

Tucker's Tree House is a magical place hidden among the eucalyptus trees just off the Freedom Trail. It is a place where children with disabilities or cancer can spend time with our puppies-in-training and be surrounded by the healing power of nature. We had a big turnout for the grand opening.

A week later, I was cleaning out my office and discovered some of my old books from school. I flipped through the pages of a binder and found some notes from when I was just starting out. And there it was—the list of rules! I scanned it and had to laugh when I realized that I had broken every one along the way. Looking back, I could see that God had a different plan than I had. By staying open to change and keeping the most important rule—not letting the fear of something bad stand in the way of doing something good—so many more doors had been opened and more lives had been touched.

The following spring, Will and I visited Wendi at the hospital with our newest hero-in-training, a two-month-old golden retriever named Quincy. Wendi had met dozens of our puppies over the years, but this time we had a surprise for her.

"There's something really special about this one," I said as she held Quincy in her arms.

Her eyes filled with tears as she looked up and said, "He's the first one that's reminded me of Tucker."

"Well, that's probably because he is Tucker's nephew!" Will said with a smile.

Wendi was overjoyed by the news and quickly began to point out all their similarities. He was gentle, just like Tucker, and had the same kind expression. His golden coat was as downy soft as Tucker's and just a shade darker. He also had a big head, huge paws, and thick ears . . . just like Tucker! Quincy lay on his back and melted into Wendi's arms as she gushed. She smiled down at him and looked into the twinkling dark eyes that she knew so well. Quincy smiled up at her . . . and burped.

Wendi took us on rounds with her that day, and we met a delightful ten-year-old girl named Ally, who had recently been diagnosed with leukemia. She sat on the hospital bed, surrounded by IV poles and monitors. Will gently placed Quincy on her lap, and her radiant smile lit up the room. Little did we know at the time that Quincy was destined to follow in his Uncle Tucker's footsteps and would become an important part of Ally's journey in the years ahead . . .

Hospital Dog Quincy and Ally

Epilogue

*Now faith is the substance of things hoped for, the
evidence of things not seen.*

Hebrews 11:1 KJV

It's been twenty years since I took a leap of faith to change
careers and follow my dream. Since then, I've had the privi-
lege of working with more than two hundred amazing dogs
and their equally incredible partners who are part of the Assistance Dogs of Hawaii ohana.

After seeing the difference these Wonder Dogs make in so
many lives, Will and I founded another program called Assistance Dogs Northwest (ADNW). It's based on Bainbridge
Island (near Seattle) and serves residents of Washington, Oregon, and Idaho.

In case you're wondering what happened with some of the
people and dogs from the stories, here's a follow-up:

Lili, the patient Tucker met on Christmas Day, fully recovered and maintained a close friendship with Tucker

throughout his life. She is currently a college student and has plans to become a pediatrician.

Dr. Wendi and Barry got married and moved to Portland, Oregon. She has a hospital facility dog named Winnie and is the director of the ADH/ADNW Crisis Response program that helps victims of mass casualties and natural disasters.

Shine On! Kids launched their own Hospital Dog program in 2018 to help meet the growing demand for hospital dogs in Japan. Our former intern, Marina, is their lead trainer.

Our first intern, Cate, became a doctor of occupational therapy and is now the director of the ADH/ADNW Hospital Dog program. She is a leading expert and sought-after speaker on the therapeutic benefits of hospital dogs and canine-assisted interventions.

Service Dog Emma has retired and is enjoying her golden years on Oahu. She still likes going to the beach every day. Rich and his family are volunteering as puppy raisers and have a puppy named Duke. He is an eight-month-old black lab— who may have already found his match! ☺

Summer and her service dog, Trooper, are still going strong and living life to the fullest. She reports that Trooper now anticipates what she wants before she can even ask for it. They enjoy frequent trips to the wine country and Las Vegas. They inspire and bring joy to everyone they meet.

Zeus is twelve years old and enjoying a life of leisure at home with Brian and his family. Zeus's hearing is failing, but he and Brian still communicate perfectly through sign language. Brian shares pictures of Zeus every day on social media.

Our first graduate, Casey, now has her third service dog, a devoted black Labrador named Wesley. Wesley assists Casey throughout the day, sometimes even when she doesn't need it. They live in Portland with her daughter and granddaughter and enjoy trips to the Oregon coast.

Quincy graduated and was placed at the children's hospital. He developed a special friendship with Ally and her family over the years. Ally is one of my personal heroes and continues to show us all what it means to be brave and strong.

Our newest heroes-in-training were recently born on Maui. They are black Labradors named Georgia, Gidget, Gigi, Gilligan, Grace, and Griffin. It is our fifth time through the alphabet naming the puppies. We are just as excited about their arrival as we were about our first puppy twenty years ago!

Will is happily putting the finishing touches on the Assistance Dogs Northwest campus on Bainbridge Island. It is a magical place surrounded by old-growth cedar forest, a babbling creek, rolling green lawns, and a duck pond. It is completely wheelchair accessible and is three acres of pure puppy heaven.

As for me, I'm currently in the midst of another research study, teaching dogs to detect the COVID-19 virus. I believe dogs still have so much untapped potential to help people in need and often wonder what will be discovered next.

To learn more about the teams in this book and watch videos of them in action, please visit our websites, www.assistancedogshawaii.org and www.assistancedogsnorthwest.org. You can also follow your favorite teams and puppies-in-training on Facebook and Instagram.

If you would like to make it possible for more Wonder Dogs to help children and adults with disabilities and other special needs, please consider supporting our mission. All donations are tax deductible and will help us to provide more assistance dogs and lifetime follow-up support free of charge.

Will and Mo Maurer with four heroes-in-training

ASSISTANCE DOGS OF HAWAII

Maureen "Mo" Maurer is the founder and executive director of Assistance Dogs of Hawaii and Assistance Dogs Northwest. Born and raised in Seattle, she holds a master's degree in canine studies. She and her husband, Will, have dedicated their lives to helping people with disabilities and other special needs with the help of their assistance dogs. Mo and Will spend their time between Maui and Bainbridge Island with their two dogs, Sadie and Samson, along with a constant stream of future heroes-in-training.

Jenna Benton is a writing coach, editor, and freelance writer from Southern Oregon. She loves research, coffee, and helping people and businesses tell their stories (not necessarily in that order). You can learn more about Jenna by visiting her website at www.jennabenton.com.

ASSISTANCE DOGS OF HAWAII

Unleashing Abilities.

Assistance Dogs of Hawaii is a multifaceted assistance dog program that has graduated over 130 teams including service dogs, hospital dogs, and courthouse dogs who make a daily difference in the lives of their partners and those they serve.

Head to **assistancedogshawaii.org** to learn more!

AssistanceDogsOfHawaii

AssistanceDogsOfHawaii

AssistanceDogsHawaii

ASSISTANCE DOGS NORTHWEST

Unleashing Abilities.

Assistance Dogs Northwest is a 501(c)(3) charitable organization that provides children and adults who have disabilities and other special needs with professionally trained dogs that will increase their independence and enhance the quality of their lives.

Head to **www.assistancedogsnorthwest.org** to learn more!

AssistanceDogsNW

assistancedogsnorthwest

assistancedogsnorthwest